SWEET SALT
NAVAJO FOLKTALES AND MYTHOLOGY

D1118482

When the Navajos were first introduced to refined sugar, they had no word for it. However they did have a word, ashiih, which it looked like, and a word for sweet, likan. They put them together and came up with ashiih likan or salt (that is) sweet, and translated into English that becomes the title of this book,

SWEET SALT

SWEET SALT
NAVAJO FOLKTALES AND MYTHOLOGY

RAYMOND FRIDAY LOCKE

ROUNDTABLE PUBLISHING COMPANY
SANTA MONICA, CALIFORNIA

For Ron Schnell
A kind man, and a friend.

Cover photograph by Marianne Greenwood
Cover design by Mitch Burkhardt
Type design by Tony Stately
Typography by Nghiêu Nguyễn

Library of Congress Cataloging-in-Publication Data

Locke, Raymond Friday
    Sweet salt.

    1. Navajo—Legends. 2. Navajo Indians—Religion.
3. Mythology. 4. Title.
E99 N3L744   1989   224   89-60774cif
ISBN 0-915677-43-1   398.1 0899774

First Edition

10   9   8   7   6   5   4   3   2   1

PREFACE

I n 1976 I published a military, social and cultural history of the Navajo people, after eight years of extensive research and writing. It was called *The Book of the Navajo*. In the autumn of 1989, the fourth edition of that book was published. I'm rather proud of that work and definitely like a review which appeared in The Boston Globe which stated, in part: "Locke writes splendidly; this is history laced with data, you-are-there commentary and poetic symbolism. He rarely minces words." Nice, huh? Even nicer was the fact that the Navajos accepted the work and it has been used as a teaching tool at the tribal run Navajo College ever since.

During the research and writing of *The Book of the Navajo* I became friends with many Navajos, individuals and often, several people in a family. You will find the names of a few of those people scattered throughout the introductory passages to the tales published in this book. Among others, they will be Manuelito Begay, Shirley Sells Teller, Elizabeth Sells, the Cato Sells family of Window Rock, Vern Teller, Gordon and Teresa Gorman, the Gorman families of Ganado and Chinle, R. C. Gorman, Larry Issacs, Jr., Billie Begay, Bill and Nancy Begay, Deswood Tome, Donald Benally, the late Ninabah Morgan Cahn and Ruth Morgan Green. Non-Navajos who supported this project in one way or another are Marianne Greenwood, Ron Schnell, Abe Kuipers, Edgar Cahn, Philip Astley-Jones, Gino and Ellen Farrone, Ralph and Elfie Weinstock, and Christopher Riccella. Some of them have been friends for more than twenty years and those who are still among the "Earth Surface People" are still friends.

Now that you've been introduced to a few of the people who matter to me, let's have a few words about what we're doing here and how I, at least, got here. In the last twenty-one years I have traveled with Navajos, eaten with them, attended their ceremonies, been lost in their deserts, been snowed in with them, laughed and cried with Navajos. A few of those memories are shared in this book which I hope is a palatable offering of Navajo folktales and mythology, with short introductory passages in which I've attempted to tell a bit about the story that follows.

I think about right here I should say that I resisted writing this book for years. The raw research material had already been collected back when *The Book of the Navajo* was originally published. As the first edition got generally good notices and was accepted among the Navajo, themselves, I had several offers from various publishers to "do anything" on the Navajo, including one from an university press for which I have the highest regard. For a long time I had no inclination to write anything more about the Navajo. However, I never really stopped going back to Navajoland, visiting and researching. I'd been hooked.

I was blessed in being able to spend most of the summer of 1982 in and around Window Rock and Tsaile while serving on an ad hoc committee chaired by Dr. Edgar Cahn of the London School of Economics. We prepared a White Paper projecting the social, economic, and cultural effect the recent Navajo Relocation Project (as it is politely referred to by non-Navajos) would have on individual families and on the tribe as a whole. During that too brief summer I had the opportunity to meet and talk to many Dineh that I'd not met before and that, much to my everlasting thanks, included two wonderful women who happened to be sisters, Ruth Morgan Green and Ninabah Morgan (who would soon afterwards become Mrs. Jonathan Cahn). Ruth had studied anthropology and Ninabah would, before her death in 1989, become the highest ranking woman in the tribal government.

They were both highly intelligent, educated women who believed in "the Beautiful Rainbow of the Navajo."

I had already started researching a book that I intend to finish one of these years that will be called *The Keepers of the Sacred Hogan* with a focus on the pre-European contact period of Navajo history in the Southwest; a task which Ruth Green shared my passion. She had collected quite a lot of material and gave me copies of her own research late in 1982. I didn't know it at the time but Ruth knew that she did not have long to live.

I first seriously considered doing this book after I got to know Ninabah and Ruth. I had already published a brief, sanitized version of the Navajo Emergence or Creation Story in *The Book of the Navajo* which seemed to meet the approval of the Navajos I discussed it with. Then one day I was in Gallup with Deswood Tome, Ruth's son, went into a book store and found a copy of a very rare book: *Navajo Creation Myth: The Story of the Emergence* by Hasteen Klah as recorded by Mary C. Wheelwright.

In discussing Wheelwright's work (you'll find more about that in the introduction to The Fifth World section of the book in hand), it was suggested that I expand on the version I'd used in *The Book of the Navajo*.

One day, it was a Sunday, we began swapping Navajo "folktales" and Ninabah and Ruth, who had been reared as traditional Navajos, began correcting versions of the tales I'd recorded. I remember Edgar Cahn being there and somewhat amazed as some of the more curious turns a few of the stories take; you probably will be also. They both encouraged me to put the tales in the form of a book as did, eventually, several other Navajos.

It certainly sounded like a good idea at the time. I put together notes, transcribed quite a lot of tapes, with the help of my friend Faye Lattimore. Still. Eventually I put the project aside and really did nothing about putting together the book you hold in your hand (and I'm not sure this is the book I started out to do in any case). Then, in the fall of 1986, Christopher Riccella, then a student at the University of Southern California, was helping me with some research and read *The Book of the Navajo* and the notes and material that was done on this project and urged me to complete it. Eventually, a contract was signed, Chris entered all the material I had into a computer and the book, only the gods know how, got done. Frankly, I was ready to give it all up several times and especially when the Bear Woman story got erased from the computer for the second time in the fall of 1989.

"Of course," said a Navajo friend. "You're not supposed to tell that story in the summer, between the first thunder storm of spring and the time when snakes hibernate."

Of course.

Raymond Friday Locke
Studio City, California
Christmas, 1989

INTRODUCTION
THE WORLD IS HOLY

This book contains a collection of what a non-Navajo would refer to as folktales. A few of them, toward the end, are just that. However, to the Navajo, all except the modern tales at the back of the book are sacred stories from religious ceremonies or Navajo "Ways" as such rites are referred to by traditionalists who follow the ancient "beauty trail" or old Navajo way of life.

The complex Navajo cosmology and the religious rites, which are essential to their way of life in maintaining harmony and balance with nature, were long ignored by white Americans and others who thought The People (Dineh, as they refer to themselves) had no form of worship at all.

The Navajos have no collective center for worship, no calendrical worship, exactly, and no word or phrase in their language which could possibly be translated as "religion." Religion is not a separate entity to be believed in or subscribed to; it is ever present. It could no more be separated from the traditional Navajo's daily life than eating, breathing, sleeping, or the earth which gives life in combination with the sun which also gives warmth or the summer lightning which gives fear. Holy rites and practices are an essential element in nearly every aspect of traditional Navajo culture, pervading it to such an extent that, paradoxical as it may seem, it was several decades before white Americans who lived among the Navajo realized they possessed any from of worship at all.

Dr. Jonathon Letterman, post surgeon at Fort Defiance in the 1850s, reported to the Smithsonian Institution in 1855: "Of their religion little or nothing is known as, indeed, all inquiries tend to show they have none; and even have not, we are informed, any word to express the idea of Supreme Being. We have not been able to learn that any perserverances of a religious character exist among them; and the general impression of those who have had means of knowing them is that, in this respect, they are steeped in the deepest degradation . . . It is impossible to learn anything from the people themselves, as they have no traditions. A volume of no mean size might be written, were all the stories of interpreters taken for truth; but it would be found a mass of contradictions, and of no value whatever."

We have no way of knowing what stories the interpreters told Dr. Letterman, but since his time a couple of dozen of volumes "of no mean size" have been written on Navajo ceremonials. What the Spanish called "the great dances of the Navajo" a hundred years before Dr. Letterman's time were profoundly sacred celebrations, as Dr. Washington Matthews, who arrived on the reservation in the 1880s, was able to learn, probably because he didn't arrive with a head filled with notions about what, exactly, constitutes holy rites.

Dr. Matthews, after several years of concentrated study of Navajo "sings" or ceremonial rites, began the publication of what eventually amounted to nearly a dozen papers and books on Navajo "religion." Father Berard Haile, who devised the first Navajo-English dictionary, wrote several substantial manuscripts each of which is devoted to one of the dozens of Navajo ceremonials; in more recent times, Leland C. Wyman, Karl W. Luckert and others have done extensive research and publication in the area of the Navajo people's relationship with their gods, which is often expressed in most elaborate ceremonials.

A volume nearing the size of the Bible can be written about just one of the complex Navajo ceremonials, and in the past they numbered somewhere between fifty and sixty, in addition to the variations. Therefore, this dissertation on the holy world of the Navajo will, of necessity, be cursory.

In the Navajo pantheon there is no distinguished deity who can exactly be described as a supreme being. Tosohanoai, the Sun Bearer (and not the sun itself; the deity is the god who carries the star across the sky and not the sun. That old saw about Native Americans worshiping "Father Sun and Mother Earth" was probably, for want of a more likely culprit, an invention of Sir Robert Baden-Powell, founder of the Boy Scouts). Sun Bearer's father Klehanoai, the Moon Carrier; Changing or Turquoise Woman (Estsanatlehi), who is associated with the earth; First Man and First Woman who created the mountains and the heavens, and the Hero Twins, Monster Slayer and Born of Water, sons of Changing Woman and her sister White Shell Woman (Yolkai Estsan) are among the more important deities. Changing Woman and White Shell Woman are one entity in some versions of the all-important Emergence Story. Other entities, or Holy People, occupy less dominant or minor positions without, however, the clear-cut divine hierarchy which characterizes the Greek or Roman pantheons.

The universe, as viewed by the Navajo, is an orderly system of interrelated elements, an all-inclusive unity that contains both good and evil. Therefore the universe is at once, good, benevolent and dangerous and, with the exception of Changing Woman, who is always benevolent, if a bit high-handed about it on occasion, the gods and holy people are themselves sometimes good, sometimes dangerous. Some entities which are described by Gladys Reichard as "persuadable deities" are predominantly good. These include figures who play an important role in the Creation Story and in the proper development of the universe for the ultimate benefit of man. Among these are Sun, the Racing Gods, First Man, First Woman, Salt Woman, Talking God and House God. While First Man and First Woman are more often than not motivated for good, they control witchcraft and through sorcery are sometimes responsible for disease and misery.

They and other deities, including the Yeis, representing forces of nature, and a group called the Mirage People who bridge the gap between the gods and the Earth Surface People (humans), figure prominently in the Navajo legends and in various ceremonials. Talking God, known both as Haste Yalti and Yeibichai, is given the honored position of "grandfather" of these Earth Surface gods and as such commands much respect and is also the god who initiates children into ceremonial life.

Navajo belief is not formalized in the familiar Asiatic-European pattern, therefore the myths and ceremonials are not embodied in a creed or formalized doctrine by the Navajos. With the Navajo concept of the universe being a state in which good and evil are maintained in interrelated harmony, the problem, therefore, is maintaining that harmony. The primary purpose of the ceremonials, sometimes called "Ways" or "Sings" after Matthews' translation of the word hatal to holy chant or song, is to keep man in harmony with the universe. Father Berard Haile concluded that "Way" was a more accurate English rendering of the word hatal and the English names for most of the many ceremonials are now suffixed with the word.

The ceremonials are conducted by a "Singer" or "Chanter" called a Hataali by the Navajos and a "medicine man" by most whites. Usually Singers know perhaps only one, or at the most two or three complete ceremonials and specialize in those. It would be impossible for one man to learn all the complicated rituals for more than a few ceremonials. In the Night Way alone, Matthews (and others have done so since) recorded 576 songs and each song must be uttered word and intonation perfect to accomplish its purpose. The Singer must also, besides remembering all the songs for a ceremonial that might last nine days, hold in mind clearly the details of the symbols and their positions, the equipment, the elaborate rituals and the dances, and direct the creation of the drypainting (which most non-Navajos call the sandpainting).

An apprentice Singer studies the rite that he wishes to learn by observing, and finally aiding, an older, respected Singer. Such apprenticeships have been known to go on for twenty years; however it is more common for the learning period to last anywhere from a third to half that. It is becoming more common for an apprentice Singer to study only a couple of years and master one of the shorter, less complex ceremonies. The common practice is for the student to pay the Singer for his teaching of the knowledge he owns—even in the case of a nephew or close relative. The Singer is said to "own" his ceremonies and songs and while he doesn't exactly sell his knowledge—that would be considered bad manners by most Navajos—gifts, including money, are exchanged, often as long as the teacher and student relationship lasts. Unfortunately, in the last few decades and mostly because of the demands of having to also exist in the "white man's world," fewer men apprenticed themselves to become Singers (and especially following World War II) and some important ceremonies were lost in their entirety and are not performed anymore.

Disease, misfortune, distress, and evils caused by failure to observe taboos and ceremonial regulations, or by natural elements or phenomena such as whirlwinds, lightning, water or weather are reasons for a ceremonial. The worst reason for having to order up a ceremonial and—considered the best reason for having one by some Navajos—is witchcraft. The Navajo people believe in chindi and while "evil" is closer to an exact translation, witchcraft does clearer get the meaning across to the English speaking person.

The belief in chindi is still widespread among the Navajo but it is a subject that is seldom discussed with outsiders. The Navajos call their witches "human wolves" or "Navajo wolves" and believe they become supernatural beings to obtain riches or revenge. Navajo wolves can be either men or women and are believed to be capable of causing illness or the death of those whom they dislike. They are said to go about at night dressed in the skins of wolves or coyotes; it is also said that they can turn themselves into wolves. To become a chindi one goes through an elaborate ceremony and pays for the privilege by designating a relative, usually a brother or a sister, as a sacrifice. Two days later the relative dies.

The belief in witchcraft was, in the past, a form of social control. If a man was stingy and grew too rich he was in danger of being accused of being chindi. Such a man, unlike most Navajos, would refuse to share his food with the hungry who came to his door, and his riches with relatives. He might also take the water supply and grazing grounds used by others without their permission. Navajos suspected of being chindi were tried by a group of respected leaders and executed in the past. A few years after the Dineh were returned from their 1860s Fort Sumner imprisonment following the war made on them by the United States, some of the young men started raiding their neighbors and caused the danger of another outbreak of hostilities between the Navajos and the American army. The respected headmen, Manuelito and Ganado Mucho, went on a "witch hunt," caught, tried and executed forty men, including Ganado Mucho's own uncle and, thereby, put an end to the troubles.

Each Navajo ceremonial, rite or Way is especially adapted to a particular set of uses, to combat or thwart one or another disease or misfortune. Or, in case of a Blessing Way or some other lesser Ways, just to put the patient—and friends and relatives who attend—back in harmony with nature.

The specific ceremony required is determined by divination, itself a ceremony and one carried out by a process of hand trembling, star gazing or listening. A Diviner interprets the involuntary motions of the hand, or the thing he or she (Diviners and Healers are sometimes women) sees or hears while in a trancelike state, and discovers the cause of the problem. Once the proper ritual for a cure is determined, the Diviner may recommend a Singer. A Diviner or Healer, as this person is sometimes referred to in early writings, is not usually a Singer, and a Chanter referred to in those same writings may not be either but is the Singer's apprentice or helper.

Once it has been determined what sort of Way is called for, the Singer is contacted and a date is set for the beginning of the ceremonial, at least four days ahead unless there is a dire emergency. Meanwhile the family of the patient must prepare for the Way; the hogan is emptied and swept clean; firewood, medicinal plants, sand, sandstone and other materials for the drypainting are gathered; grinding stones, baskets, buckskins and calico must be provided and much food prepared for the vistors. Members of the family and the extended family, and possibly others, visit throughout the ceremonial but on the final day and night of a Way it is not unusual for a hundred or more people to show up. A very big "sing" such as the Mountain Way given by a well known family will attract hundreds of people.

The Singer's "gift" is always made in advance. The cost of a one or two night rite may be the equivalent of fifty or a hundred dollars but a great nine day ceremony such as the Mountain Way may cost a couple of thousand dollars. A lengthy curing rite sometimes taxes the finances of the entire extended family. Incidently, the Mountain Way is always open to outsiders but they should behave themselves as they would at any sacred rite. Non-Navajos are sometimes invited to other Ways, such as the Blessing Way, but attending without an invitation is considered very bad manners.

During the many curing Ways, the patient is purified through rituals and eventually becomes identified with the deities whose help is sought to restore him and put him back in harmony with the universe. It has been pointed out that the sense of security the patient derives from the host of relatives and friends who surround him during the ceremony is also conducive to his recovery. Herbs and native medicines are administered to the patient during many of the ceremonials for his physical well-being. During the past couple of decades many white doctors on the reservation have recognized the psychological benefits of the native ceremonies and it is no longer unusual for a Singer to visit a patient in one of the modern hospitals either at the invitation of the administrators or with their permission.

The curing chant Ways are always concerned with some specific disease. Hail Way and Water Way treat illness resulting from cold or rain. The Shooting Chant is used to cure injuries received from lightning—rare, but somewhat more common in the Navajo's part of the world than most of the rest of the country—and from arrows (gunshot wounds, nowadays) or snakes which are cognate to lightning or arrows. Snakes are also an important etiological factor associated with Navajo Wind Way and Beauty Way. Beauty Way is also used to combat aching feet, legs, arms, back and waist, swollen ankles, itching skin and mental confusion. Insanity, very rare among the Navajos, and paralysis require the Night Chant.

The Night Chant, commonly referred to as the Yeibichai, is a major ceremony that may be given only between the first frost of autumn and the first thunderstorm of spring, when the snakes are in hibernation and there is no danger from lightning. Of all the Ways, this nine-day ceremonial is the most frequently given, but it must be carried out in minute detail and in exactly prescribed order. Sometimes, of course, winter weather will interfere and make this very difficult.

The Navajos believe that a mistake either by the Singer or the patient during its performance can result in crippling, paralysis or a loss of sight or hearing. Both boys and girls, at some time between the ages of seven and thirteen, are initiated into participation in the ceremonial life of the adults on the last night of a Night Way. Two masked figures, Yeibichai or Haste Yalti, grandfather of the gods, and his divine helper, appear heralded by Yeibichai's Hu Hu Hu Hu call.

Each of the boys to be initiated, naked to the waist, is in turn led out into the firelight, where one of the masked figures places sacred white corn pollen on his shoulders, while another impersonator of the gods strikes him with a bundle of reeds. The girls, in turn, are marked with sacred yellow corn pollen. Finally these awesome creatures remove their masks, revealing to the initiates that they are not the gods themselves but human impersonators, known to the children. The masks are then placed on the face of each child in turn. It is said that the child then sees the world as it is seen through the eyes of the gods.

After the initiation ceremony, the long Yeibichai dance begins, usually with twelve or more dancers taking part, and continues for the remainder of the night. When dawn breaks everyone, vistors and performers alike, stand, face the east and repeat the Prayer of Dawn. When the prayer is finished, the Bluebird Song is heard. The bluebird is the symbol of happiness and heralds the break of day:

> Just at daylight Bluebird calls.
> The Bluebird has a voice
> His voice is melodious
> That flows in gladness.
> Bluebird calls, Bluebird calls.

The creation of drypaintings, often incorrectly called "sandpaintings," is an integral part of almost all ceremonies. There are five required during the Night Way. Among almost all the Native Americans of the Southwest, the drypainting is an important part of curing rites. No other people, however, have developed this art to the degree the Navajo have. The People recognize between

600 and 1,000 separate designs of drypaintings. There are thirty-five different paintings for the Red Ant Way alone. Most often the Singer directs the "painters" but does not directly participate in the creation of the drypainting. However, he holds an exact picture of the painting as it should be done in his mind and quickly corrects a crooked line or some other mistake no matter how slight.

The painting is created on sand or sometimes on cloth or buckskin with, of course, sand, corn meal, flower pollen, powdered roots, stone and bark. Because of the sacred nature of the ceremony, the paintings are begun, finished, used and destroyed within a day, usually before nightfall. The purpose of the painting is curative and it is believed the patient, by sitting upon the representation of the Holy People depicted in the drypainting, will become identified with them and absorb some of their power.

At the conclusion of the ceremony, the sands and other materials of the drypainting are carefully gathered upon the buckskin or a blanket. The Singer then walks east, then south, then west and north. With symbolic gestures up to the sky and down to the earth, he scatters the sands to the six directions from whence they came. Sometimes those present are given a small amount of the sacred sand. In some ceremonies all the sand is buried.

A drypainting may be a simple affair of three or so feet wide (the photograph on the cover of this book was taken just before one of that size, a minor curing ceremony, was executed in Monument Valley), or may be as large as twenty feet long and almost as wide and require several assistants to execute. The paintings that are executed during a sacred ceremonial follow a prescribed sequence and Singers seldom allow photographs to be made. On the other hand, because of the desire of white Americans, particularly, to see a "sandpainting" they are often done for exhibition purposes at Indian fairs. In the latter color and direction are often reversed and other "mistakes" deliberately made. Traditional Navajo Singers consider the creation of authentic drypaintings for exhibition purposes a profanity.

For the same reason a complete relating of the Navajo myths that accompany the Ways to an outsider is considered to be profane by many Singers. Therefore, there is no "official" version of the all-important Story of Creation or The Emergence Story (told in The Lower Worlds, The Separation and The Fifth World in this book). Certain details vary from one Singer to another and, more important, depending on the circumstances of the telling. In recent years, as in the case with my first teacher, Manuelito Begay, knowing and respected Singers have come to realize that certain ceremonies have been lost already and others are in danger of being forgotten because no apprentice Singers are studying them. Passing them on to be recorded and written down, therefore, is one way to preserve them. Some of the "myth-tales" as Washington Matthews called them, which I've related in this book are composites of two, three or in a couple of cases, even more versions I've heard. I've also always cross checked the tales with those gathered by Matthews a century ago for the simple reason that his versions of the important tales are very similar to those I've collected, and are the most coherent to the English reader.

The story of the Dineh's emergence into this world, and the events that followed shortly thereafter are told in the Navajo ceremony, the Blessing Way. This legend, actually a series of "myth-tales" was said by Dr. Matthews to be the Navajo's version of his history before the Europeans came to the Southwest.

The Navajo myths are not only the basis of the complex ceremonials, they are also the history of the Navajos, much as the Old Testament is both the Judaic religious base and the history of the ancient Jews. The New Testament is not only the history of the first Christians, it is the foundation of Christianity. Hence, the Navajo myths are, in fact, the Navajo's version of his own history. The all-important Story of Creation or Emergence Story, is retold in its entirety in the Blessing Way and in other Ways as well, much as a rabbi might instruct his congregation in the Book of Moses or a priest might read the story of Christ to his flock.

In making this comparison during a college lecture once, I was challenged by a student who said, "Yes, but the Judaic and Christian religions were based on written books." Well, not in the beginning, they weren't. The laws and history of the Jews were oral history for several centuries before they were written down by Jews who were being held captive in Babylonia c. 400 BC, and it was two to four hundred years after Christ that the New Testament was put down in written form.

The first part of the Navajo Story of Creation parallels the Biblical book of Genesis in that it tells of the creation of the world. In fact the Navajo concept of the world is not unlike the early Judaic-Christian concept which described the earth as a land area floating in an immense ocean overspread by a solid domed heaven which fit like great lid with its edges on the horizon, resting on supports in the water. Above the sky was still another similarly domed world. The Navajo Story of Creation (The Lower Worlds in this book) traces the evolution of life through four such underworlds until The People emerged in this, the fifth and present world. As The People passed through each of the first four worlds, they went through a process of

evolution, starting out as insects and finally becoming people as we know them today in the fourth world—with the
explicit aid of certain holy beings. Above this world there
is yet another world where all things blend into one with
the cosmos.

Subsequent events in the Navajo Story of Creation and
other legends, with a loose stretch of the imagination, may
be made to parallel Biblical stories. The expulsion of the
Insect People from the first world for committing adultery
parallels Adam and Eve's expulsion from the Garden of
Eden; the destruction of both the First World and the
Fourth World by flood might, of course, be compared to
the story of Noah; and the slaying of the monsters of the
Fifth World by the Hero Twins can, with a wide stretch
of the imagination, be compared to David slaying Goliath.
Such parallels, however, are coincidental and should not
be used, as has been attempted, to find a common root
for the Navajo Story of Creation and the Old Testament.

The Navajo legends are an oral history of the Dineh that
has been passed down from Singer to Singer, father to son,
from generation to generation. There are, as I've said, variations in the tellings as there must be in any oral history,
but the variations are slight (with a couple of exceptions
and those will be discussed in the introduction to The Fifth
World Emergence Story); the characters are also always
the same, though they are, as in the case of Estsanatlehi
(Changing Woman, also called Turquoise Woman) and
her sister, Yolkai Estsan (White Shell Woman) sometimes
interchangeable. But this is an abstraction that is perfect-
ly clear to the Navajo.

Dr. Washington Matthews conducted his studies of the
Navajo "myth-tales" before the Dineh were overly exposed to the influence of white teachers and missionaries who
often altered the legends and taught them to Navajo

children to fit within a quasi-Christian concept. Too, some white students of Navajo history and anthropologists have made changes in some of the legends which caused them to conform to a personal thesis.

For example, it was not until recent years that the theory of the Navajo's recent migration from the north was questioned in spite of the fact that the Navajos—those who chose not to believe the "migration" theory taught them by white teachers—have maintained the legend of a much earlier migration from the west. Not wanting to dispute academia's theory of a southward migration of Athapascan-speaking people, some writers have written a version of the origin myth that expediently left out the Navajo's version of an eastward migration.

Both Dr. Washington Matthews and Frederick Webb Hodge stated that, omitting a few obvious mythical elements, "the Story of Creation and subsequent Navajo legends can be substantiated by recorded history" long before there was archaeological evidence that at least parts of the story are credible. For example, a Navajo Singer told Matthew in the 1880s that traditionally all his people believed their ancestors arrived in the area around Chaco Canyon, New Mexico, when the Anasazi were in the process of building pueblos there. It wasn't until Dr. Andrew E. Douglass developed the dating process known as dendrochronology (tree-ring dating) in 1929 that we were able to attach dates to the massive ruins in Chaco Canyon. Thanks to Douglass' work, we now know that the oldest section of the ruins date from about AD 900. Building continued in Chaco Canyon until about AD 1130.

A few years ago ruins of Navajo type hogans were uncovered near Gallup, south of Chaco Canyon, and in Northwestern New Mexico and Southwestern Colorado, north of the canyon. These were dated by archeologists at c. 1100, giving credence to the Navajo's claim of arriving in the area at about the time the Anasazi (a Navajo word meaning "old ones") were building their pueblos there. And not several hundred years later, at about the time the Spanish themselves first arrived in the middle of the sixteenth century as was supposed by those same Spanish and, later, American historians.

Today about one hundred and sixty thousand Navajos live in the Navajo Nation which encompasses about twenty-four thousand square miles of rugged, semi-arid land in the states of Arizona, New Mexico and Utah. This is only about one-third of the land they called Dinetah and which they controlled prior to the 1860s. The reservation, which is about the size of the state of West Virginia, is crowded and several thousand Navajos spill over into adjacent lands, some of which are owned by individuals and others by the Navajo tribe. This includes the nearly ten thousand who were "removed" from their homelands a few years back in the infamous "Navajo-Hopi Land *Dispute*," which I discuss at length in *The Book of the Navajo* and Jerry Kammer tells the story of in his book *The Second Long Walk.*

Dinetah, as the Navajos still call their homeland, is a land of flat alluvial valleys where stretches of sagebrush are interspersed with groves of pinyon and juniper trees; of rolling upland plains and high pine and aspen clad mountains and brightly colored mesas. In this land deep mysterious gorges and towering cliffs of spectacular beauty abound. But it is also a hard land, and farmers still depend upon irrigation to grow crops of corn, beans, pumpkins and melons much as they did hundreds of years ago.

Here and in adjacent lands evidence has been found of the earliest known habitation of man in the Western Hemisphere. Here, too, about two thousand years ago evolved what is recognized as the first American Indian civilization in what is now the continental United States, that of the Anasazi. It was to this land that a wandering tribe of mysterious origins came about a thousand years ago. Once they came into contact with the Anasazi, they settled down and became tillers of the soil, and as much a part of this beautiful land as the deep red canyons and tall pine trees of its mountains. In Navajo legends their ancestors married with the Anasazi, and many elders of the Dineh believe until this day they are the lineal as well as the spiritual descendants of the mixture of the wandering Athapascans and the Anasazi.

Over the centuries the Navajos have come to love their harsh, beautiful homeland, that land of the beautiful rainbow with which their ancestors learned to live in harmony. In harmony at least, with their kind. The Navajos fought and successfully resisted the Spanish and their Indian allies for almost three hundred years in what amounted to a continuing war, and they most often held the upper hand. Their war with the United States lasted for two decades and in the end they were not just defeated, they were a beaten people, starved into submission and eight thousand of their number—men, women and children—were marched three hundred miles across New Mexico and imprisoned for four long years. During their imprisonment those that survived subsisted on the most meager rations imaginable; usually rancid pork fatback and weevily flour deemed unfit to be eaten by their soldier guards. Taken from their burning hogans—a shelter that is warm in the winter and cool in the summer—by Kit Carson, who led an army of New Mexico volunteers, regular army, Utes and other Indian allies against them, they were given no shelter in return at their Bosque Redondo prison, near the Texas state line on the Pecos River. Almost overnight a people with a culture far in advance of that of any of their neighbors was turned into a nation of beggars, living in the open and eating coffee beans and raw flour to stay alive. Their gods, they said, had deserted them.

Finally the Navajos were returned to a small portion of their beloved homeland because the United States government was tired of feeding them and, at the end of the Civil War, they simply did not know what to do with eight thousand Navajo prisoners of war. They returned to the land they called Dinehtah pitifully poor, ill of body and ill of soul. They had signed a treaty promising to remain at peace forever for which, in return, they were to receive token replacements for their sheep and other livestock that had been systematically killed by Carson's soldiers, and an American teacher for every thirty children as the powers in Washington thought it important that they become "civilized." The Navajos kept their part of the treaty in spite of the great temptation to retaliate against the New Mexico neighbors who had caused most of their problems, and who continued to make raids on them after the peace treaty. From that low point in their history, a hundred and twenty years ago, the Navajos have, primarily through their own effort, recovered to a great extent. The Navajos survived through an innate sense of "oneness" that compels them to help each other both in times of wealth and in times of poverty.

The following song is not from one of the ancient ceremonies but is said to have come into being after the Dineh were, finally, allowed to return home again after the four years of imprisonment at Bosque Redondo. It is said that on their walk west, towards Dinetah that, upon reaching the Rio Grande and seeing sacred Mount Taylor in the distance, old men fell to their knees and cried. And one of them thought up the words to this song:

"This is your home, my grandchild!"
He says to mew as he sits down beside me;
"My grandchild!
"I have returned with you to your home,"
He· says to me as he sits down beside me;
"Upon the pollen figure I have returned
  to sit with you, my grandchild!"
He says to me as he sits down beside me;
"You homes are yours again—
"Your fire is yours again—
"Your food is yours again,
  my grandchild,"

He says to me as he sits down beside me.

To the Navajo all is holy, the world is holy. People who visit Dinetah should always keep that in mind. Parts of ceremonies and "sings" and drypaintings are staged at the various fairs held in and around the reservation. It is even possible to be escorted to a portion of a War Way ceremony if you're visiting Navajoland in the summer.

The third night of the War Way, a curing ceremony in which the disease is treated as the enemy nowadays but in former times was held for warriors returning from raids or contact with the enemy—or too close association with any non-Navajo, for that matter—is popularly known as a "Squaw Dance." It is the only ceremony at which couples dance. A summer ceremony, it may be held any time after the beginning of summer rains and until harvest time, or when the first frost announces the arrival of the season of the great winter Way celebrations. Young women, most often with a demeanor of great disdain, choose the men they will dance with and the only way for the male to avoid dancing until he drops is to pay her off. And handsomely, too. A few dollars is often enough for a man to ransom himself but if the lady decides that the offer is too little, tough. The male keeps dancing until either he has paid an amount which meets her approval, or she grows totally disgusted with him. Actually, it is all in fun but still a certain protocol must be followed.

I'd taken the liberty of writing a short introduction to the "myth tales" that follow. In some cases the story has special meaning to me as does, in particular, the story of The Maid Who Becomes A Bear, the first story in the book. Others, I felt, needed a bit of explanation. It is my hope that this introduction to Navajo "folklore" will serve as an introduction to a wonderfully unique culture that co-exists within the bounds of the major white American (or Anglo, as the Navajos would put it) culture. For over a hundred years now there have been those who have attempted to cause the Navajos to forget their past and their gods out of ignorance and religious zeal.

That cannot be allowed to happen. My hope is that this effort will help prevent that.

THE BEAR WOMAN

The story of "The Maid Who Becomes A Bear" (Tsike Sas Natlehi) is one of my favorite tales from The Story of Creation, a mythological saga of epic proportions that has been called the "Bible" of Navajo mythology. My first exposure to Bear Woman's story was studying the works of Washington Matthews as a college student. I first heard the story told—and was able to record it—by the Singer Manuelito Begay in the late winter of 1972. The story was translated from Navajo to English by his nephew (or grand nephew). It is a Fifth (or present) World story and falls near the end of the creation story.

The story of Maid Who Becomes A Bear brings to mind a couple of memorable trips to Dinetah. In the summer of 1975 I took one last research trip to the Southwest in preparation for the completion of the first edition of The Book of the Navajo and, as had been planned the prior summer, connected in Santa Fe with Abe Kuipers, of Holland, who had been exposed to Navajo and their beautiful land only in books up until that time. From there we traveled by train to Gallup for our rendezvous with

Shirley Sells and Richard Johnson, who were at that time married. After dinner that evening we ended up at The Esquire Lounge, then about the only respectable "Indian Bar" in Gallup. Among the customers was a rather large (she was easily over six feet tall) woman who was quite attractive and carried herself with grace and dignity. I had encountered her in the same place about five years earlier. She was called "Bear," after the maiden of the story, for reasons that will become obvious.

We, with the exception of Abe, knew when she'd had too much to drink and got peeved about something or other, she'd been known to wreak havoc on any and all private and/or public property that caused her displeasure—and that included both civilians and those who worked in a law enforcement capacity.

That evening, as time wore on and considerable alcohol was consumed, she became most taken with Mr. Abe Kuipers of Friesland. For the second time, while under the influence, she'd taken a notion that she wanted to "marry" one of my friends from Europe (the other had been the Swedish diarist/photographer Marianne Greenwood). We eventually got Abe rescued from his Bear Maiden and into an automobile speeding back to the safety of Window Rock.

The next morning we four piled into a new Audi and headed for Monument Valley by way of Bluff, Utah. At Mexican Water, Richard suddenly remembered a wagon trail that supposedly ran directly across the desert to the San Juan River and Bluff. Twenty miles and two hours later, Shirley, Abe and I were out of the car, walking in front and searching for a trail for Richard to follow in the Audi. It was August 1st—my birthday—hot as blue blazes and the reason Richard got to drive in air conditioned comfort was because the car belonged to his sister. And neither Shirley nor I wanted to be held responsible for having to abandon it wherever Richard's "short cut" stranded us. Eventually we came upon an isolated hogan and an old Navajo woman who directed us to a trail that actually led us to the San Juan River and Bluff (if we had a reason for wanting to go to Bluff, a small town of large Victorian houses and few trees, I certainly don't remember what it was). But I never think of the Bear Woman story without remembering that August 1st and the evening before spent with a Frieslander and three Navajos, one of them a woman called Bear.

A second Bear Woman story involves a bitter cold winter night, and my friend and researcher, Christopher Riccella.

And a blizzard.

New Year's Day, 1987, Christopher and I flew to Phoenix and picked up a rental car. Our planned destination was a Night Way Ceremony that was being held somewhere between Chinle and Many Farms in a few days, and a world away from the Fiesta Bowl and a football game between Penn State and Miami for the national collegiate championship, which was our first stop. A few minutes after we arrived in Window Rock on a Sunday afternoon it started snowing. By the next morning there was several inches of snow on the ground and more was falling, preventing us from doing much of anything but hang out at the motel restaurant I affectionately call "The Navajo's Revenge." Tuesday morning we stopped by the BIA offices to say hello to my friend, Elizabeth Sells, and then headed for Chinle, some sixty-five miles away. We made a couple of stops and didn't arrive until mid-afternoon. It was already dark—the dark of an approaching storm—and beginning to sputter snow. And the weather report from Flagstaff was predicting fourteen to sixteen inches of snow that night. We checked into the Thunderbird Ranch Lodge and waited for the storm to arrive. We had about a thirty minute wait. We were in the cafeteria eating the "daily special," an opened-faced beef sandwich smothered in a red sauce. Chris was speculating on the origins of that sauce—"a true Navajo revenge"—when the storm hit with the force of a tornado. First it became very dark and that was followed by a blizzard front that was hellish white. While literally fighting our way back to the room across a parking lot, I made a reference to it being "Bear Woman weather."

Trapped in a motel room in the middle of the Navajo Nation with the damnedest blizzard I'd ever experienced—the official count where we were measured eighteen inches—and nothing on television but station WGN, Chicago and some woman on that blabbering about tenement fires and robberies, I took the opportunity (at his urging) to tell Chris the story of Bear Woman. I eventually fell asleep but he insists he stayed awake all night, expecting Bear Woman to come crashing through our single window—the one the drape wasn't quite large enough to hide us from her view in case she was prowling about. The storm stayed around a couple of days, as did Bear Woman as far as Chris was concerned. And so did we, trapped in the new and very motel-like wing and eating at the very Americanized cafeteria.

The first time I'd seen Canyon de Chelly was a wonderfully cool August in 1969. I was there with Marianne Greenwood and they still served meals family style in the old building that held living quarters for the help and the "cafeteria" building was the trading post. I was introduced to it by Marianne, and had the good fortune of having as a guide to the canyon a Navajo College student and forest ranger named Larry Issacs Jr., who would later earn his doctorate in law and is now in charge of Indian Education for Eastern United States. I quickly grew to share Larry and Marianne's love for Canyon de Chelly, still the most magical place I know of. Larry allowed me to discover a couple of hard facts about the canyon: dry sand there often covers a quicksand trap; Mummy Cave is probably haunted (on that Marianne and I certainly agree) and, yes, there are bears in the canyon. I've always, since, associated Canyon de Chelly with the spiritual and with bears.

Eventually we got back to Window Rock with Chris driving through still another blizzard and on to Flagstaff where we experienced another "Bear Woman" night.

The Bear Woman story, like most of those that appear in this collection, is a composite and, except for a rather randy description of Bear Woman and Coyote's wedding night that is told by some Singers, is as complete as I know how to make it.

BEAR WOMAN STORY

This is the story of how the most beautiful woman among all the Dineh (Navajo) came to marry Coyote, fell under his spell, turned herself into a ferocious bear and did much harm to her family. This is the story of Bear Woman.

In those times, after the Dineh (Navajo) had entered this, the Fifth World, people were not like they are today. Some were like the present day Skin Walkers (witches) in that they could assume the shape of animals. And some animals, especially Coyote, could also assume the shape and form of a human. Coyote, of course, was a divine being, having come to be in the Fourth World.

Coyote came among us in the following manner. When The People had been expelled from the First World for their transgressions; then from the Second World for the same reason, and, yet again from the Third World, because they still hadn't learned to behave themselves, they entered the Fourth World, which was very much like this Fifth (and present) World of the Navajo.

It was, of course, in this Fourth World that the Navajo came upon the Kisani (Anasazi, or Pubelos) for the first time. And when many of the divine creatures were created, including man in the form we know him today. It was in this Fourth World that the gods also created First Man (Atse Hastin) and First Woman (Atse Asdzan), from whom all the Dineh are descended but that is another story and not of importance in this one.

At any rate when the People had been in this Fourth World of the Pueblos for eight years, and had married among the descendents of First Man and First Woman and no longer resembled their old selves, this strange thing happened, which they all saw.

One day they observed the sky stooping down and the earth rising up to meet it. For a moment the earth and the sky came into contact and they coupled.

Then sprang out of earth, at the point of contact, Coyote who was soon followed by Badger. The Coyote rose first, and for that reason he is the elder brother of Badger and they both are children of the sky.

Now, as you will learn, Coyote caused a lot of mischief and much trouble for the People in the Fourth World and, indeed, was the cause of them being expelled from there. Still, he came with the Dineh into this, the Fifth World but he did not change his ways. If anything, once he got here, he only became more adept at stirring up mischief and causing trouble.

In those days after the ancient ancestors of our mothers (Anasazi) built the great houses at Chaco Canyon, there lived over near the Chuska Mountains (running north to south along the Arizona-New Mexico border), a maiden of renowned beauty who was the sister of twelve divine brothers. She had been sought in marriage by many men: warriors, leaders and great hunters. Her refusal had attracted the attention of Sun God and other gods who had also sought to marry her but they, too, had been refused.

It was while Coyote was visiting his friend named Yelapahi (Brown Giant), one of the Naye'i (the monsters, or alien gods) that he heard of this beautiful maiden who had refused all of her suitors because of certain conditions she had imposed that none of them could meet. One day, leaving Brown Giant to work on a sweat house, he went to visit the maiden.

"Why have you refused so many powerful gods who have asked you to be their wife?" asked Coyote of the maiden after he had greeted her.

"It would profit you nothing to know as you would not be able to comply with even one of my demands," she replied.

Four times he asked and three times he got the same reply. However, when he asked for the fourth time she answered, "In the first place I will not marry anyone who has not killed one of the Naye'i." When he heard this reply Coyote arose and quickly began his journey back to the home of Brown Giant who, of course, was one of the Naye'i.

On his way back he found the thigh bone of one of the great animals who once roamed thereabouts and concealed it under his shirt. Upon his arrival he found that Brown Giant had finished the sweat house. Coyote suggested they enter and take themselves a sweat bath because a plan to benefit himself and help him gain as a wife the beautiful sister of the twelve divine brothers had come to mind.

"You are a very slow creature," Coyote said to the

Brown Giant. "Your enemies taunt you terribly and take you to be a fool because you cannot run fast."

"This I know," replied Brown Giant. "But what can I do?"

Truly, Brown Giant had often pondered this problem but as a Naye'i, one of those creatures who had sprung from the blood of the monsters the women had given birth to for their transgressions in the lower world, he was as slow as the lava, the leftover blood that had formed the great lava beds near Grants, New Mexico.

"Well, Yelpahi," said Coyote, "I want to be your friend, therefore I will help you to learn to run fast and overcome the spell put upon you by your blood which is slow, like lava. Now, you look at me. As you have seen, I can run fast and jump far; I can jump over four bushes at one bound. Through my magic I can teach you to run fast and catch your enemies, as I am able to do.

"My cousin," responded Yelpahi, "You can do me this favor if you will."

"Gladly, my friend," replied Coyote, smiling so broadly that his gleaming teeth could be seen in the darkness of the sweat house.

"Why do you grin so?" asked Brown Giant.

"Because it makes me so happy to be able to help you, my friend," replied Coyote.

"Now," he continued, "if you want to be able to run fast, I will show you what to do. You must cut the flesh of your thigh down to the bone and then break the bone. It will heal again in a little while and when it heals you will be stronger and swifter than ever. I often do this myself and each time I do it I am fleeter of foot than I was ever before. I will do it now, so that you may observe how it is done."

Coyote then pulled a great stone knife from where he

carried it in a pouch on his legging and pretended to cut his own thigh, wailing and crying and pretending he was suffering great pain. After carrying on in this manner for some time, he put the old femur on top of his thigh, held it by both ends and said to Yelapahi: "I have now cut to the bone. Would you care to feel it, my friend?"

The giant then put forth his great hand and felt the bone in the absolute darkness of the sweat house.

"That is enough," Coyote said, pushing the giant hand away, "I must rush because to go slowly about things is not my way and it could do damage to my magic."

Quickly, Coyote struck the bone several times very hard with the stone knife until it broke with a loud cracking sound.

Then he told Brown Giant to feel the fractured ends, which he did and was very much in awe of Coyote's braveness in breaking his own bones.

Again Coyote pushed the giant hand away and said, "Enough! I must hurry with my magic." Then he concealed the pieces of old bone beneath an animal skin rug that was on the floor. Next he prayed and sang and in a little while presented his sound thigh to the giant to be examined, saying: "See! My limb is healed again. It is as well as ever and now I will be able to run faster and jump even higher than before! This is the magic I use to outwit my own enemies."

Then he handed the knife to Brown Giant and the latter, with many tears and loud howls, slowly amputated his own thigh. When the work was done he put the two severed ends together, spat upon them, sang and prayed as Coyote had done.

"Stick! Stick! Stick!," he cried.

"Heal together! Grow together!" he commanded, but the severed ends would not reunite.

"Cousin," he called to Coyote, "help me heal this leg."

But instead of helping Yelapahi, he ran from the sweat house, seized his bow and arrow and discharged his arrows into the helpless Brown Giant, who soon expired of his wounds.

Coyote then scalped his victim, took the quiver and weapons of the slain and set out for the lodge of the beautiful maiden. He knew she would recognize the scalp of Yelapahi for the alien gods had yellow hair such as no other people had in those days.

When he reached the hogan of the maiden he said: "Here is the scalp and here are the weapons of one of the Naye'i. Now you must marry me."

"No," said the maiden, "not yet; I have not told you all that one must do in order to win me. He must be killed four times and come to life again four times."

"Do you speak the truth? Have you told me all?" asked Coyote.

"Yes, I speak only the truth," she replied four times, as Coyote asked the question four times. In that manner, as is the Dineh custom, she placed her honor and that of her family in jeopardy if she later recounted, or had not told the truth.

Satisfied, Coyote said: "Here I am. Do with me as you will." The maiden then took Coyote a little distance from the lodge, laid him on the ground, beat him with a great club and left him for dead. But she had not smashed the point of his nose or the tip of his tail where, unlike other beings, he kept his vital organs.

She returned to the lodge and went about her work, of which she had much to do, but she had hardly begun her tasks when she looked up and saw Coyote standing in the door. "Here I am," he said. "I have won one game; there are only three more to win."

This time she took him farther away from the lodge and pounded him to pieces with her club. She threw the pieces away in different directions and again returned to her work.

She had taken but a few stitches in a basket she was making when Coyote again appeared in the doorway saying: "I have won two games; there are only two more to win."

Again she led him forth, taking him even farther away from the lodge, and with a heavier club she pounded him into a shapeless mass, until she thought he must certainly be dead. Then she took the mass to a great rock and there she beat it into still finer pieces which she scattered in all directions as she had done before and went back to the lodge. But she had still failed to injure the two vital spots. It took Coyote a longer time to pull himself together but again she had not wrought much on her basket when he presented himself and said: "I have won three games, there is but one more game to win."

The fourth time she led him farther away than ever. She not only mashed his body to pieces, but she mixed the pieces with earth, ground the mixture like corn between two stones until it was but a fine powder and scattered the powder far and wide. But again she had neglected to crush the point of the nose or the tip of the tail. She went back to the lodge and worked for a long time undisturbed. She had just begun to entertain hopes that she had seen the last of her unwelcome suitor when he again entered the door.

Now she could not refuse him. He had fulfilled all her conditions so she consented to become his wife. He remained in her hogan all afternoon making love to his bride. At sunset they heard the sound of approaching footsteps and she said: "My brothers are coming. Some of them are evil of mind and may do you harm. You must hide yourself." Then she hid him behind a pile of skins and told him to keep himself quiet and make no noise.

When the brothers entered the lodge the elder of them said to their sister: "Here is some fat young venison which we bring you. Put it down to boil and put some of the fat into the pot for our faces are burned by the wind and we want to grease them."

The pot was put on and the fire replenished but when it began to burn well an odor denoting the presence of some beast filled the lodge. One of the brothers said: "It smells as it some animal has been in the wood pile. Let us throw out this wood and get fresh sticks from the bottom of the pile." They did as he desired, but the unpleasant odor continued to annoy them, and again the wood was taken from the fire and thrown away. Deciding that the whole pile of wood was tainted with the smell they went out, broke fresh branches from trees and built the fire up again, but this still did not abate the rank odor in the least. Then one said: "Perhaps the smell is in the water. Tell us, little sister, where did you get the water in this pot?"

"I got it from the spring where I always get it," she replied. But they told her to throw out the water and fill the pot with snow, and to put the meat down to boil again. In spite of all their pains the stench was as strong as ever.

At length one of the brothers turned to his sister and said: "What is the cause of this odor? It is not in the wood. It is not in the water. Where does it come from?" She was silent. He repeated the question four times, yet she made no answer. But when the question had been asked the fourth time, Coyote jumped out of his hiding place into the middle of the lodge and cried: "It is I, my brothers-in-law!"

"Run out of here!" the brothers commanded, and turning to their sister, they said: "You leave here with him if you are truly his wife!"

As Coyote ran from the lodge, with his wife following him, he took a brand from the fire and with it he started a new fire. Then he broke boughs from the nearby trees and built a shelter for himself and his bride to live in. When this was completed she went back to the lodge of her brothers and, took out her pots, skins, four awls, baskets, and all her property and carried them to her new home.

One of the elder brothers said to the youngest: "Go out tonight and watch the couple and see what sort of a man this is that we have for a brother-in-law. Do not enter their shelter, but lie hidden outside and observe them." This he did, and while he watched Coyote killed his wife four times and each time she was resurrected. After the fourth time she lay down and Coyote followed her to the couch. From time to time during the night they held long, low conversations which the youngest brother of the woman could not hear. At dawn, when he returned to the lodge, he said: "I cannot tell you all that I saw and heard, and they said much that I could not hear, but what I did hear and behold was evil."

The next morning when the twelve divine brothers started out to hunt, Coyote came and asked if he might join them, but they told him to stay home with his wife as she might get lonely and need someone to talk to. Then they chased him away and left. But they had not gone far when he overtook them. Three times they chased him back, but on the fourth try they consented to take Coyote along. At the edge of a canyon they made a bridge of rainbow, on which they proceeded to cross the chasm. Several tribes of dangerous creatures who owned evil magic lived in the canyon and were to be avoided.

Before the brothers reached the opposite bluff, Coyote

jumped on it from the bridge of rainbow, with a great bound, and began to frolic around, saying: "This is a nice place to play."

They left him there and traveled farther on. After awhile they came to a mesa where they observed the tracks of four Rocky Mountain sheep. Coyote finally caught up to them and they sent him out into the brush to drive the sheep to them, which he did. The sheep were all killed and presently Coyote returned.

In those days the horns of the Rocky Mountain sheep were flat and fleshy and could be eaten. The eldest brother said: "I will take the horns for my share."

"No," said Coyote, "the horns shall be mine. Give them to me." Three times each repeated the same declaration. When both had spoken for the fourth time, the eldest brother, to end the controversy, drew out his knife and began to cut one of the horns. As he did so Coyote cried out, "Turn to bone! Turn to bone! Turn to bone!" Each time he cried the horn grew harder and harder and the knife slipped as it cut, hacking but not severing the horn. That is why the horns of the Rocky Mountain sheep are now hard, not fleshy, and to this day they bear the marks of the hunter's knife.

The hunters gathered the meat all into one pile and by means of the mystic powers that they possessed they reduced it to a very small mound which they tied into a small bundle such as one person might carry and gave it to Coyote to take home. They warned him to travel back home the way they had come and not cross through the canyon they had avoided as an evil people dwelt there. They also told time not to open the bundle until he got home.

Of course Coyote promised to heed all that he had been told, but as soon as he was well out of sight of the hunters he slipped the bundle off his back and opened it. At once the meat expanded and became a heap of formidable size, such that he could not bind it up again and carry it; so he tied up as much of it as he could carry and left the remainder scattered on the ground, then continued on his journey. And of course, being foolishly inquisitive, he entered the forbidden canyon.

When Bear Woman's brothers returned home without her bridegroom, Coyote, she came to them and looked about inquiringly.

"Where is my handsome new husband?" she asked.

The eldest brother told her: "Go back to sleep and don't worry about that worthless man of yours. He is not with us and we do not know what has become of him. We suppose he has gone into the canyon where we warned him not to go and has been killed."

She became very angry and returned to her lodge.

Before the brothers lay down to sleep they again sent the youngest brother to hide and watch their sister, and this is what he saw that night: At first she pretended to go to sleep. After awhile she rose and sat facing the East. Then she faced in turn the South, the West, and the North. When she had done this, she pulled out her right eyetooth, broke a large piece from one of her four bone awls and inserted it into the place of the tooth, making a great tusk where the little tooth had once been. As she did this she said aloud: "He who shall hereafter dream of losing a right eyetooth shall lose a brother." After this she opened her mouth to the four points of the compass in the order in which she had faced them before, tore out her left eyetooth and inserted in its place the pointed end of another awl. As she made this tusk she said: "He who dreams of losing a left eyetooth shall lose a sister."

Then she made, in the same manner, two tusks in her

lower jaw. When she had made the one on the right she said: "He who dreams of losing this tooth (right lower canine) shall lose a child." And when she had made the one on the left she said: "He who dreams of losing this tooth (left lower canine) shall lose a parent."

As she began to pull out her teeth hair started to grow on her hands, and as she went about her mystic work the hair spread up her arms and her legs, leaving only her breasts bare. Finally the hair grew over her breasts and she was covered with a coat of shaggy hair like that of a bear. She continued to move around in the direction of the sun's course, pausing and opening her mouth at the East, the South, the West, and the North in turn. After a time her ears began to wag, her snout grew long, her teeth were heard to gnash and her nails turned into claws. The youngest brother watched her until dawn; then, fearing he might be discovered, he returned to his lodge and told his brothers all that had happened.

They said: "These must by the mysteries that Coyote explained to her their wedding night."

A moment after the young man finished telling his story they heard the whistling of a bear and soon a great female bear rushed past the door of their lodge, cracking the branches as she went. She followed the trail that Coyote had taken the day before and disappeared in the woods.

That night she returned, groaning. She had been in the forbidden canyon all day fighting those she presumed to be the slayers of Coyote and she had been wounded in many places. Her brothers saw a light in her hut and, from time to time, one of them would go and peep through an aperture to observe what was happening within. All night she walked around the fire and, at intervals, by means of her magic, drew arrowheads out of her body and healed the wounds.

Next morning Bear Woman again rushed past the lodge of her brothers and again went off toward the forbidden canyon. At night she returned as before, groaning and bleeding, and again spent the long night in drawing forth missiles from her body and healing her wounds by means of her magic.

Thus she continued for four days and four nights, but at the end of the fourth day she had conquered all her enemies. She had slain many and those she had not killed she had dispersed. The swallows flew up into the high cliffs to escape her vengeance; the otters hid themselves in the water; the spiders retreated into holes in the ground, and in such places these creatures have been obliged to dwell ever since.

During the four days Bear Woman had journeyed to the fatal canyon and slain her enemies, the brothers remained at home, but at the end of that time eleven of them left. It was now deep winter and they had to track farther for game. They divided themselves into four parties, one of which traveled to the east, another to the south, another to the west and the last to the north. They left the youngest brother at home to guard the lodge.

When they were gone, the Whirlwind and the Knife Boy came to the lodge to advise the youngest brother. They dug a hole for him in the center of the hogan, and from this they dug four branching tunnels, running east, south, west and north, and over the end of each tunnel they put a window of gypsum to let in light from above. They gave him four weapons, the chain-lightning arrow, a stone knife as big as the open hand, the rainbow arrow and the sheet-lightning arrow. They roofed his hiding place with four flat stones, one white, one blue, one yellow, and one black. They put earth over all of these, smoothing the dirt and tramping it down so that it looked like the natural floor of the lodge. Then they gave him two monitors, Nich'i, the Wind, at his right ear to warn him by day of the approach of danger, and Chahalgel, Darkness, at his left ear, to warn him by night.

When morning came and Bear Woman, having healed herself for the fourth night in a row, discovered that her brothers were gone she was very angry for she still blamed them for the death of her husband. She poured water on the ground to see which way they had gone. The water flowed to the east; she rushed in that direction and easily tracked her brothers in the light snow that had fallen the night before. She overtook them, catching them unawares, and easily killed her brothers.

Then she returned and again poured water on the floor. It flowed off south so she followed in that direction. A winter storm slowed her but still she overtook and killed three more of her brothers. The next time it flowed to the west and following in that direction she lost her way several times as a second storm, much stronger than the one of the day before, held her back. Eventually she overtook and killed three more of her brethren. The fourth time the water flowed to the north, and going in that direction, she encountered a fierce blizzard that blew for four days and four nights yet she was still able to overtake and kill the two older of her brothers. She returned to the lodge and poured water on the ground to see what had become of her youngest brother. The water sank directly into the earth.

She scratched all around the lodge of her brothers, working her way toward the center. Here she found that the earth was soft, as if recently disturbed. She dug rapidly downward with her paws until she came to the stones and, removing these, saw her remaining brother hidden beneath them.

"I greet you, my younger brother! Come up, I want to see you," she said in a coaxing voice. Then she held out one finger to him and said: "Grasp my finger and I will help you up."

But Wind told him not to grasp her finger as she would throw him upward, he would fall at her feet and be at her mercy.

"Get up without her help," whispered Wind.

He climbed out of the hole on the east side and walked toward the east. She ran toward him in a threatening manner, but he looked at her calmly and said: "It is I, your younger brother." Then she approached him in a coaxing way, as a dog approached one with whom he wishes to make friends, and she led him back toward the deserted hogan. But as he approached it Wind whispered: "We have had sorrow there, let us not enter," so he would not go in. This is the origin of the custom the Navajos have of never entering a house in which a death has occurred or where a great misfortune has taken place.

"Come," Bear Woman said, "and sit with your face to the West and let me comb your hair."

"Heed her not," whispered Wind. "Sit facing the North so that you watch her shadow and see what she does. It is thus that she has killed your brothers." They both sat down, she behind him, and she untied his queue and proceeded to arrange his hair while he watched her out of the corner of his eye.

Soon he observed her snout growing longer, approaching his head, and he noticed that her ears were wagging. "What does it mean that your snout grows longer and that your ears move so?" he asked. She did not reply but drew her snout in and kept her ears still. When these changes had taken place four times, Wind whispered in his ear: "Do not let this happen again. If she puts out her snout the fifth time she will bite your head off. Yonder, where you see that chattering squirrel, are her vital parts. He guards them for her. Now run and destroy them."

He rose and ran toward her vital parts and, with a snarling howl, she ran after him. Suddenly, between them, a large yucca sprang up to retard her steps, and then another cactus of a different kind. She ran faster than he, but was so delayed in running around the plants that he reached the vitals before her and heard her lungs breathing under the pinon that covered them. He drew forth his chain-lightning arrow, shot it into the weeds, and saw bright red blood spurting up. At the same instant Bear Woman fell with blood streaming from her side.

"See!" whispered Wind, "the stream of blood from her body and the stream from her vitals flow fast and approach one another. If they meet she will revive and then your danger will be greater than ever. Draw, with your stone knife, a mark on the ground between the approaching streams." The young man did as he was told, and the blood instantly coagulated and ceased to flow.

Then he turned to his sister and said: "You shall live again but no longer as the mischievous Bear Woman. You shall live in other forms, where you may be of service to your kind and not a thing of evil." He cut off the head and said to it: "Let us see if in another life you will do better. When you come to live again, act well, or I will slay you again." He threw the head at the foot of a pinon tree and it changed into a bear, which at once started to walk off. But presently it stopped, shaded its eyes with one paw and looked back at the man, saying: "You have bidden me to act well but what shall I do if others attack me?"

"Then you may defend yourself," said the young man, "but begin no quarrel and be ever a friend to your people, the Dineh. Go yonder to Black Mesa and dwell there."

Next the hero cut off the nipples and said to them: "Had you belonged to a good woman and not to a foolish witch, it might have been your luck to suckle men. You were of no use to your kind but now I shall make you of use in another form." He threw the nipples up into a pinon tree, heretofore fruitless, and they became edible pine nuts.

Next, with the help of his friends, Whirlwind and Knife Boy, he found the corpses of his brothers and brought them back to life. They went back to the place where the brothers had dwelt before and built a new house. They could not return to the old hogan for it was now a place cursed by death.

All this happened a very long time ago at a certain place up near Tsaile.

THE LOWER WORLDS

W here we now live, this "earth surface world," is the Fifth World of the Navajo Cosmos. A sixth world beyond this is told of in Navajo mythology and some informants say there are eight worlds all together while it is said by a few others that there are twelve worlds in all.

The first four of these worlds are flat on the surface, covered by a large dome that is the sky, the under surface of which is extremely hard. These worlds are stacked one on top of the other, like inverted bowls. It is said that all eight (or all twelve) worlds are "the same way."

The beings that started out in the First World were insects (the Insect People) and, gradually, as they moved from world to world, these creatures evolved until, in the Fourth World, they took on human form—with the help of certain gods. The Navajo Story of Creation or The Emergence Story as it is sometimes called, is both a tale of evolution and creation. The various worlds seem to have existed "from the beginning" while beings both evolve and are changed at the will of the gods. Or created by gods, as in the case of First Man (Atse Hastiin) and Atse Asdzan (First Woman). First Man and First Woman, in turn, are able to change the world by creating mountains, the sun, moon, stars and so forth but almost always with the help and advice of others. I feel that I've used a more acceptable version of the Creation Story here. However, in some versions of the story, First Man and First Woman, along with Coyote and numerous other beings, already existed in the First World, while people are created from ears of corn in the Fourth World. Here, the temptation to draw parallels with biblical stories is very strong— certainly, I've done it as have most people who have written about the Lowerworlds, or Creation Story, or Emergence Story of the Navajo.

Biblical parallels are justified in comparing Navajo religion with that, presumably, of the non-Navajo reader and, really, for no other reason. A few have done so to manufacture a common source thesis which is actually unnecessary and, in any case, a waste of time and effort. There is no way to easily and comfortably explain Navajo mythology in terms of the European culture based experience. I've never seen a reason to attempt to do so.

THE FIRST WORLD

The First World was an island, surrounded by oceans, and there lived the first beings who started out in life. Although these beings are referred to as "people", they were not people as we now know them but were insects and, therefore, they are called the Insect People.

The Insect People were twelve in number: Dragon Flies, Red Ants, Black Ants, Red Beetles, Yellow Beetles, Hard Beetles, Black Beetles, White Faced Beetles, Dung Beetles,

Bats, Locusts and White Locusts.

These Insect People lived in dwelling places on the borders of three streams in the middle of this First World, all of which emerged from a central source. Two streams flowed to the south and one flowed to the north. Dragon Flies, Red Ants and Black Ants lived on the south flowing stream to the right; the various tribes of beetles lived on the south flowing stream to the left; while the locusts lived on that stream that flowed to the north. Bats dwelled in the high cliffs that bordered this north stream.

In this First World, the surface of which was red in color (some versions give the color as black), white rose in the east and the Insect People regarded it as day there; blue arose in the south and they still regarded it as day, but when yellow arose in the west they knew that evening had come; then black arose in the north and the Insect People lay down to sleep. There was neither sun, moon, nor stars in this First World.

In the oceans that surrounded the First World dwelled the four Gods of the Insect People. These gods were Tieholtsodi (Water Monster) who lived in the ocean to the east, Tgaltl'a Galle' (Blue Heron) who lived in the ocean to the south, Ch'al (Frog) who lived in the ocean to the west and Adini Dzil (White Mountain Thunder) who lived in the northern ocean.

The four gods soon became angry with The People and this is the way it happened: These Insects, being the first people created, were primitive and knew nothing of clans and clan laws. So they committed adultery, one sort of Insect People with the other, and as a result were constantly quarrelling and fighting amongst themselves. Tieholtsodi, God of the East, observed the Insect People and said: "What shall we do with them? They do not like the land in which they dwell or they would not behave in such a manner. . . "

In the south Tgaltl'a Galle' warned them of the consequences of their conduct, telling them they'd best behave themselves. Ch'al (Frog) who ruled the West observed that they were not acting right and Adini Dzil warned that if they did not learn to behave themselves they would no longer be welcome where he ruled.

Still The People continued to act badly and quarrel amongst themselves until it came to pass that none of the gods would speak to them.

Again they copulated, one sort with another, causing even more violent disagreements among these First People until Ch'al lost all patience with them and said: "Go elsewhere at once. Leave here!"

Then Adini Dzil said: "Go elsewhere and keep on going," as he, too, was through with them. But the Insect People paid no attention to the warnings of their gods and continued to do the same things until finally the gods held a council that lasted all night to decide what they must do with these people who refused to listen to reason.

At dawn Tieholtsodi called to The People and said: "You pay no attention to our words. Constantly you disobey, therefore you must go to some other place. Not in this world shall you remain."

For four nights the women of the Insect People talked about what the gods had said but as they knew of no other place but this one they came to no decision. Besides they still could not agree on anything so they did nothing. At the end of the fourth night, as morning dawned, The Insect People saw something white appear in the east. Then it also appeared in the south. Next it appeared in the west, then the north. It looked like a wall of white, as high as mountains and without a break, surrounding them. And soon, as it came closer, they saw what the white was. It was a great wall of water, impassable and insurmountable, flowing toward their world from every direction.

The Insect People had no choice but to leave the First World. They flew around in circles until they reached the sky, which was smooth and hard. When they looked down they saw that the water had risen and covered the First World. While they were flying around, wondering where they could go now, a creature having a blue head appeared in the sky above them. He saw the trouble they were in and called to them: "In here, to the east there is a hole." They entered the hole and emerged on the surface of the Second World.

THE SECOND WORLD

The surface of this world was blue in color and the blue creature who had brought them there was a cliff swallow and belonged to the Tgashji'zhidine (Swallow People) who inhabited this, the Second World. About the surface of this land were scattered their houses which were also blue in color, rough and lumpy and tapered toward the top where there was a hole for entrance. A great many of the Swallow People gathered around the strangers. They stared but had nothing to say to them.

Now since the Insect People were being watched but told nothing, they began to wonder what was in this strange Second World. When darkness came, the people from the lower world made a camp for themselves. The Swallow People went home.

The headmen of the Insect People held a conference and decided to send out two couriers, a Locust and a White Locust, to find out if there was anything here other than the Tgashji'zhidine and their lumpy little dwellings made

47

of dried blue mud. The couriers went to the east first and at the end of two days they returned and said that after one day's travel they had reached the edge of the world that was the top of a great cliff that arose from an abyss the bottom of which they could not see. They had seen no people like themselves; nothing had they seen in fact but bare, level ground, all of which was colored blue.

Then the Locust and the White Locust were sent to the south, to the west and to the north but each time they returned at the end of the second day and told The People that they had again reached the edge of the world and, again, had seen nothing but flat, level ground of a blue color. Then the Insect People knew that they were in the center of a vast barren wasteland where there was no food, nor kindred people.

It was after the couriers had returned form their last journey that the Swallow People came into the camp of the Insect People and asked them why they had sent out the couriers.

"We sent them out," was the reply, "to see what was in this land, and to see if any people like ourselves dwelled in it."

"And what did your couriers tell you?" The Swallow People asked.

"They told us that four times they had come to the edge of this world and four times they returned, yet saw no plant or river, mountains, nor streams. They had seen nothing of people or other creatures. In fact they had seen no other living thing in all the land."

"They spoke the truth," the Swallow People said. "Had you asked us in the beginning what this land contained we would have told you and saved you all your trouble. Until you came, no one has ever been in all this land but ourselves."

The Insect People considered their situation and then said to the Swallows: "You understand our language and are somewhat like us. You have legs, feet, bodies, heads and wings, as we have. Why cannot your people and our people become friends?"

"Let it be as you wish," replied the Swallows, and both people began at once to treat each other as members of one tribe; they mingled one among the other, and addressed one another by the terms of relationship, such as "my brother," "my sister," "my father," "my mother," "my daughter," and "my son".

The Insect People and the Swallow People lived together in the Second World in harmony for twenty-three days. But on the night of the twenty-fourth day one of the Insect People made too free with the wife of the chief of the Swallow People. The next morning, when the chief found out what had transpired in the night, he said to the strangers: "We have treated you as friends as you requested and look how you have returned our kindness! We doubt not that for such crimes you were driven out of the lower world, and now you must leave this world. This is our land and we will have you here no longer. Besides this is a not a good place for you. It is a barren land and without substance. You Insect People will soon perish here even if we spare you."

When the Swallow chief had finished speaking, the Locust took the lead and soared and circled. He was followed by all the Insect People and again they flew upward until they reached the sky.

But they found the sky of the second world like that of the first, smooth, hard, and impossible to penetrate. They circled around under it, looking for a way to get through until they saw a white face peering out at them. It was the face of Nilch'i', the Wind. He told them that if they would fly to the south they would find a slit in the sky through which they might enter the Third World. They did as they were told and found the opening in the sky, which slanted up toward the south. They flew through the slit into the Third World.

THE THIRD WORLD

Now, the color of this Third World was yellow and the creatures inhabiting this place were the Grasshopper People who, like the Swallow People, gathered around the strangers but said nothing. The Grasshopper People lived in holes in the ground along the banks of a great river which flowed through their land toward the east. Again the Insect People sent out the Locust couriers, to see what was in this Third World. The Locusts explored the land to the east, to the south, to the west and to the north, but returned from each journey after two days, saying they reached the edge of the world and found no kindred people in it, nor anything else but a barren land in which no people lived except the Grasshoppers.

When the Locust couriers returned from their fourth and last journey, the two great chiefs of the Grasshoppers visited the strangers and asked them why they had sent out explorers. Again the strangers answered that they had sent out the Locusts to see what was in the land and if there were any people like themselves living in it.

"And what did your couriers find?" The Grasshopper chiefs asked.

"They found nothing but a barren land in which there is nothing but a river and peopled by none save yourselves."

"There is nothing else in this land," said one of the

Grasshopper chiefs. "Long we have lived here, but we have seen no other people but ourselves until you came here."

As the strangers had spoken to the Swallows in the second world, they now spoke to the Grasshoppers, pointing out that they spoke the same language and were alike in many ways and begged that they might remain and become one people with them. The Grasshoppers consented to allow the strangers to stay and at once the two peoples mingled among one another and embraced one another, and called each other by the endearing terms of relationship, as if they all belonged to the same tribe.

As before the strangers were treated with great kindness and lived happily among the grasshoppers for twenty-three days, but on the night of the twenty-fourth day one of them served a chief of the Grasshoppers as the chief of the Swallows had been served in the Second World. In the morning, when the wrong was discovered, the Grasshopper chief called the strangers around him and said: "I suppose you were chased from the world below for such sins. You shall drink no more of our water, you shall breathe no more of our air. Begone!"

Again the Insect People flew upwards and circled around and around until they came to the sky but, as before, they found it hard, smooth, and impenetrable. When they had circled around for some time, looking for an opening in the sky of the Third World, they saw a red head appear out of the sky. It was the head of Red Wind and he told them that if they would fly to the west they would find an opening.

The passage which they found in the west was twisted round like the tendril of a vine as it had been made by the wind. They flew in circles through it and came out into the Fourth World. Four of the Grasshoppers came with them: one white, one blue, one yellow and one black and that is why there are grasshoppers of those four colors.

THE FOURTH WORLD

The surface of the Fourth World was mixed black and white. The colors in the sky of this world were the same as in the lower worlds but there was little of the white and yellow; the blue and the black lasted most of the time. And still, in the Fourth World, there was neither sun, moon nor stars.

The strangers saw no living beings in the Fourth World when they arrived but they could see four great snow-covered peaks sticking up at the horizon—one to the east, one to the south, one to the west and one to the north.

Again the Locust couriers were sent out to see what this world contained. Journeying to the east first, they return-ed after two days to report that they had traveled far but had been unable to reach the eastern mountain—and that they had seen no sign of life. Next they journeyed south and again returned after two days. The couriers related that they had reached a low range of mountains but had been unable to reach the great peak. And while they had seen no living creatures, they had seen two different kinds of tracks, such as they had never seen before. The tracks they saw and described were those made by the deer and the turkey.

Again two couriers were sent to the west but they return-ed after two days, having failed to reach the western peak, nor had they seen any living creature or sign of life. Then the couriers were sent to the north. When they returned from their journey of two days they related that they had failed to reach the northern peak but they had found living creatures. The creatures were a race of strange men who cut their hair square in front, who lived in houses and cultivated fields. These people were engaged in gathering the harvest of their fields, the couriers said, and treated them most kindly, giving them food to eat.

The day after the return of the couriers from the north, two of the newly discovered people visited the camp of the exiles. This strange race of men were the Kisani (Pueblos) and the two visitors guided the strangers to a stream of water. The water was red and the Kisani told the wanderers that they must not walk through the stream, for if they did they would injure their feet. Then the Kisani showed them a square raft made of four logs—a white pine, a blue spruce, a yellow pine and a black spruce— on which they might cross the stream to visit the homes of the Kisani on the other side. This they immediately did.

Now this land of the Kisani had neither rain nor snow but the people who lived in it raised crops of corn, squash and pumpkins by irrigation and shared their harvest with the strangers. The wanderers held a council among themselves and decided that since the Kisani had treated them kindly and fed them, they would mend their ways and do nothing to make their newly found friends angry. They lived on the food the Kisani gave them daily and all was well in the Fourth World.

Late in autumn, after the exiles had been in the new world for some time, they heard the distant sound of a great voice calling in the east. They listened and waited, and soon the voice called again, this time nearer and louder. The third time the voice called it was louder than before and closer still, and the fourth time it called the voice was louder still and clear, like the voice of one near at hand. A moment later four strange, mysterious beings appeared before them.

These four beings were Sits'is' Lagai, or White Body, a being similar to the god of this world whom the Navajos call Hasteyalti; Sit'is' Dotl'ish, or Blue Body, who was like the present Navajo god Tonenili, or Water Sprinkler; Sits'is' Li'tso, or Yellow Body, and Sit'is' Lizhin, or Black Body, who was the same as the present Navajo god of fire, Hastezhini.

Now these beings did not speak to the wanderers but made many signs, as if instructing them—none of which The People understood—then left. When these gods had gone, The People long discussed the mysterious visit, and tried to determine what the gods meant by the signs they had made. In the same manner the four gods appeared for four days in succession and made signs to The People which they were unable to understand. But on the fourth day, when the other three had departed, Black Body remained behind and spoke to The People in their own language and this is what he said:

"You do not seem to understand the signs that these gods make to you, so I must tell you what they mean. They want to make more people, but in form like themselves. You have bodies like theirs, but you have the teeth, the feet, and the claws of beasts and insects. The new creatures are to have hands and feet like ours. But you are unclean and you smell badly. Have yourselves well cleansed when we return; we will come back in twelve days."

On the morning of the twelfth day The People washed themselves well. The women dried themselves with yellow corn meal, the men with white corn meal (yellow corn belongs to the female, white corn to the male. This rule is observed in all Navajo ceremonies). Soon after the ablutions were completed, they heard the distant call of the approaching gods. It was shouted as before, four times, nearer and louder with each repetition—and after the fourth call, the gods appeared. Blue Body and Black Body each carried a sacred buckskin. White Body carried two ears of corn, one yellow, one white, each of which were completely covered with kernals.

The gods placed one of the sacred buckskins on the ground with the head to the west on which they put the two ears of corn, with their tips to the east. Under the white ear they placed the feather of a white eagle and under the yellow ear they placed the feather of a yellow eagle. Then they spread the second buckskin, with its head to the east, over the corn and told The People to stand at a distance and allow the wind to enter. The white wind blew from the east and the yellow wind blew from the west, between the skins. While the wind was blowing the Mirage People (supernatural beings) came and walked around the objects on the ground four times, and as they walked the eagle feathers, whose tips protruded from between the buckskins, were seen to move. When the Mirage People had finished their walk the upper buckskin was lifted; the ears of corn had disappeared. The white ear of corn had been changed into a man, the yellow ear into a woman. It was the wind, the Navajos say, that gave them life. When the mouth wind ceases to blow, we die. In the skin at the tips of our fingers we see the trail of the wind; it shows where the wind blew when our ancestors were created.

The pair created from the corn were First Man (Atse Hastiin) and First Woman (Atse Asdzan). The gods directed The People to build an enclosure of brushwood for the pair. When the enclosure was finished, First Man and First Woman entered it, and the gods said to them: "Live together now as husband and wife."

At the end of four days nadleeh (who were both male and female but not entirely either) twins were born, and at the end of four more days a boy and girl were born,

55

who in four days grew to maturity and lived with one another as husband and wife. First Man and First Woman had, in all, five pairs of twins—the first of which only were barren, being nadleeh.

Four days after the last pair of twins were born, the gods came again and took First Man and First Woman away to the east where the gods dwelt, and kept them there for four days. And when they returned all their children were taken to the same place and kept there for four days. First Man, First Woman and their children were taught many things in the eastern mountains. Soon after they returned they were seen occasionally to wear masks such as Hasteyalti (Talking God) and Hastehogan (House God) wear now, and when they wore these masks they prayed for all good things, such as good crops. It is thought, too, that during their visit among the gods they learned the awful secrets of witchcraft for the witches always keep such masks with them and marry those too closely related to themselves.

When they returned form the eastern mountains the brothers and sisters separated; and, keeping the fact of their former unlawful marriages to each other secret, the brothers married women of the Mirage People and the sisters married men of the Mirage People. They kept secret, too, all the mysteries they had learned in the eastern mountains. The children grew to maturity in four days, were married, and in their turn had children every four days. This numerous offspring married among those who had come from the lower worlds, as well as among the Kisani, and soon there was a multitude of people in the land.

These descendants of First Man and First Woman made a great farm, the seed for which were given to them by the Kisani. (In other versions they stole the seeds from the Pueblos.) They built a dam and dug a wide irrigation ditch.

But they feared the Kisani might injure their dam or their crops, so they put one of the nadleeh twins to watch the dam and the other one to watch the lower end of the field. The nadleeh who watched at the dam invented pottery. He made first a plate, a bowl, and a dipper, which were greatly admired by The People. The nadleeh who lived at the lower end of the farm invented the wicker water bottle. Others made tools for farming such as hoes from the shoulder blades of deer, axes of stone and implements from thin split boards of the cottonwood tree which they shoved before them to clear the weeds out of the land.

Still others, hunters among them, killed deer and one among them thought that perhaps they might make a mask from the skin of the head of the deer, by which means they could approach other deer and kill them. But they were unable to make the mask fit until the gods returned and showed them how it should be made, how the motions of the deer were to be imitated, and explained to them all the mysteries of the deer hunt. Making use of the knowledge the gods had taught them, the hunters went out the next day and killed several deer, from which more masks were made and more men were able to join the hunt. After that time The People had an abundance of meat and dressed themselves in garments made from the deerskins.

First Man was the chief of all these people who lived in the Fourth World, except the Kisani, who had their own chief. He was a great hunter and a wise man. He told The People the names of the four mountains that rose in the distance. They were named the same as the four mountains that now bound Navajoland. There was Tsisnaajini (Mount Blanca), Sacred Mountain of the East; Tsoodzil (Mount Taylor), Sacred Mountain of the South; Doko'oosliid (San Francisco Peaks), Sacred Mountain of the West; and Dibentsaa (Mount Hesperus), Sacred Mountain of the North. He also told them of the different tribe of people who lived in each of the sacred mountains.

All these strange and wonderful things having happened in this Fourth World, you would have thought The People would have been happy there. There was plenty to eat, they had become in form like the gods, there was no trouble with other people as the Kisani wished them well and offered only friendship to them.

Yet there was those about to give them trouble. These two were, of course, Coyote and First Woman. They were close in friendship and troublemakers, both of them. Not long after Coyote and Badger were created when the sky leaned down and embraced the earth, as you recall, and Nahashcd'id, the Badger, not finding this Fourth World to his liking, went down the hole that led to the lower world, Coyote took upon himself to instruct First Woman in the matters of reproduction. This was before the birth of the nadleeh and other twins produced by First Woman and First Man and this is the way it happened.

Coyote came to First Woman and complimented her greatly on her new self now that she looked as the gods did. She was very flattered and asked Coyote if he didn't also find First Man's looks pleasing.

Coyote agreed but pointed out that it was a pity there would be no more people created in their form.

"What do you mean?" First Woman asked.

"These gods can't be bothered showing up and making more people whenever you need or desire to have more. You must learn some things for yourself. You must learn to make more people yourself."

First Woman paid close attention because, obviously, Coyote was a divine being, having been born of an union between the sky and earth. Then Coyote showed her how to make a penis of turquoise and a vagina of white shell. The first he called aziz and the vagina was called joosh. Coyote told her what she must do next. She placed them on the ground and told the aziz and the joosh that they must concentrate on each other and nothing else, to block all else but the other object from their minds. The aziz was the better at concentrating because it immediately became erect and extended itself toward the joosh which had stiffened only a little. And that is why a man's desire for reproduction is so much stronger than a woman's is today.

Eventually First Woman came to see the wisdom of Coyote's instructions: The aziz and the joosh felt overwhelming desire for each other. Therefore, she decided, each man must be given aziz and each woman joosh. She first gave them to herself and First Man and the result was the nadleeh and other twins. But, of course, since Coyote was involved in all this, it would lead to trouble.

THE RIVER OF SEPARATION

One of the most important tales in Navajo mythology is the story the Dineh refer to as "The Separation" and recalls a quarrel between First Man and First Woman that led to a separation of The People by gender. It is a tale that, certainly, in former times, was used as a method of social control by males. Still, today, a Navajo man is liable to say to a wife who is threatening to leave him: "Remember what happened the last time you women tried that?"

Of course the female remembers if she's a traditional Navajo; she's been told the story all her life.

The immediate causes of this far-reaching disagreement between First Man and First Woman are commonplace. But it has been suggested by some students of Navajo mythology—and I concur—that there as a deeper meaning to the quarrel and separation. The Athapascan ancestors of the Navajo were a hunting and gathering society when they arrived in the Four Corners area. Quite suddenly these people whose lifestyle basically revolved around following migrating game and ripening seeds, found themselves among people—the Anasazi, or Kisani as they are always referred to in Navajo tales—who had built and were building what were, certainly to their woodland eyes, cities.

Perhaps the Navajo were much like they are today; in modern times they've become quite adept at borrowing what they find useful from other societies and rejecting what they have no use for. It certainly wouldn't have taken the women of these Athapascan-speaking people long to see that their new Anasazi neighbors enjoyed a much better quality of life than they did. No doubt—and this is borne out in later tales in this volume as well as in archaeological evidence—that original contact came about in the Chaco Canyon area. Historically, women had cared for the children and the home and in most hunting and gathering societies the entire tribe labored to take advantage of the short time the ripening seeds permitted. Therefore, year in and year out, substance was the responsibility of the all-important male, who hunted for the major portion of food.

The theory is that with the change to an agriculture society from a hunting and gathering people within no more than two or three generations after encountering the Anasazi, the very fabric of the beliefs and customs of those early Navajo was completely rewoven.

Prior to the contact (c. 900-1100 AD) the Athaspascan women traditionally possessed the home and all that was in it, including infants. However, her responsibility for male children ended early on, when the boy was ready to begin learning the ways of the hunt from his father or other adult male relatives. With the addition of farms, an extension of the home in reality, the woman's position within the family and tribal power structure was greatly elevated. The Navajo became a matriarchal society. And remain so until this day. Traditionally, Navajo women own the hogan, farms, grazing land, and the children belong to her clan.

In old days to divorce a husband all she had to do was place his saddle outside the hogan which sent him packing back to his mother's holdings. Too, it is within the Separation Story that one finds the beginnings of the Navajo mother-in-law taboo. In traditional Navajo society, a woman was, by custom, urged to avoid visiting her daughters when their husbands were home. In a strict sense they were not to converse with or even look upon the faces of their sons-in-law.

Once at Canyon de Chelly, I was present when a camper-tourist asked Larry Issacs, Jr. during a campfire question-and-answer period following a lecture on Dineh culture why he supposed the Navajos had such a custom. Larry's reply was simple, direct, and to the point: "It keeps a lot of trouble out of the family." Much to everyone's amusement, the Bilagaana allowed as how that was one Navajo custom he could easily learn to live with.

While it is supposed, and logically so, that the women easily adapted to the Kisani culture, the Athapascan men, on the other hand, would have found it difficult to accumulate into the Anasazi-dominated society. Not having yet developed full governmental, social, or religious structures—or learned such from their new friends—the mens' resentment, especially towards their own women, increasingly grew. Where once they were the "great hunters" of their woodland society, they now found themselves confronted with an overwhelming socially superior culture to which their women were having few problems adjusting. Although the game from their hunts still greatly supplemented familial well-being, hunting was no longer the focal point of family life.

In effect, this made the produce of women more important in sustaining the family.

Over a period of years, after the encounter with the Anasazi society, the role of the Athapascan male had become so slight as to reduce many of them to slaves—as we shall see in two later stories. This brought about a chasm within Navajo society that has for centuries been illustrated by the story of the River of Separation.

The Separation Story that follows reflects the new and perplexing role men found themselves playing once the hunting-and-gathering society went through the transition to an agrarian one. Men resented their lesser role in society, while women were becoming at least as equally important to the family unit. Even weaving became the "property" of women in Navajo society whereas among the Kisani men were often the better weavers.

The men found a way, albeit, a most drastic one to get back. To tell the truth I've "cleaned up" this version of the Separation Story somewhat. Nevertheless, the few people who saw the manuscript in advance—let me correct that, the few non-Navajos who saw the manuscript in advance—were put off by this story as being "sexist" and to say the least, "unfair to women." Well, tough. That's the way the story goes because that is the way the Navajos remember "how it happened." The Navajos who saw the book in advance, as one dear friend put it, expressed concern about my "mellowing."

SEPARATION STORY

First Woman gave birth to children, with only male offspring being mentioned, after entering this, the Fourth World, as Coyote had earlier instructed her in the ways of having sex. Some say that he also taught her about witchcraft but others say that she and First Man learned about such things when the gods took them off in those days to learn more about being of the Earth Surface tribe of people (human).

She and the other women learned how to grow and harvest food, and found life much easier than it had been before. Because they had more time on their hands now, the women were able, after a time, to pick up and come to own such crafts as weaving, pottery making, fashioning of hoes and plows and preparation of newly field-grown foods from the nadleeh who, it is said, were taught such things by certain gods. However white people, I'm told (said the informant), say it was from the Kisani mothers that the women learned such things.

At any rate, it is said that one day First Man returned from a very long and tiring hunt bringing with him a fine, fat deer that he had killed, and for which he felt very proud of himself. First Woman made a fine venison stew of the meat and corn meal which had come from their own fields and they enjoyed a bountiful meal. When they had finished eating the woman wiped her greasy hands on her dress, belched and said, "Thank you, my vagina."

"What is that you said?" asked First Man.

She repeated what she had said.

"Why do you speak in this manner?" he asked. "Was it not I who killed the deer whose flesh you have eaten? Why do you not thank me? Was it your vagina who killed the deer?"

"Yes," she replied. "My joosh is a great hunter. If it were not for that, you would not have killed the deer. If it were not for that you lazy men would do nothing. It is for want of that you men hunt and bring food to us women. It is my vagina that does all the work."

First Man said no more that night. He lay awake thinking on how ill his wife had treated him, and how badly
the house was being kept of late. The children had also
suffered from her neglect. At length he jumped across the
fire and spent the rest of the night by himself in silence.

First Man contemplated on the things his wife had said.
He also thought on how she had become self-indulgent
and neglected his family. There must be a reason for such
behavior, he thought. So the next day he decided to secret-
ly stay home from the hunt in order to follow First Woman
to see what she was doing with all her time.

Early the next morning First Man hid himself so as to
watch his wife without being noticed. At first it seemed
she was going about her usual business. Then he saw her
look around as if checking to see if anyone was about to
notice what she was up to. Quickly she went back into
their hogan returning with her finest blanket of rabbit fur.
I wonder what she is doing with that? he thought.

First Woman then concealed herself in her blanket and
began walking toward the river, a river known for its mystic
properties. Following her and concealing himself in the
reeds that grew there by the river, First Man watched as
his wife began working the evil magic that she had learned from Coyote in the lower world. Soon the waters of
the river began to churn and from the depths of the
darkness emerged Tieholtsodi, the water monster.

As she continued to work her magic, Tieholtsodi began
to turn himself into a handsome man who could live on
the surface of the earth. Her husband watched as she lay
her blanket down on the river bank to spend the day with
her lover.

First Man had seen enough. He returned to their hogan
and waited for his wife to come home, which she did not
do until dusk.

"Where have you been, my wife?" he asked.

"I have been visiting my mother, Woman Chief. She is ill," she replied, staring at the top of the trees off to the north. Aste Hastiin asked his wife four times where she had spent the day and four times she replied that she had been visiting her mother, Woman Chief, who she said was ill but the last time she replied, she lowered her eyes to the ground. First Man became very angry and boxed his wife's ears. She protested and ran from him, whereupon he picked up a stick and slapped at her legs.

"Be gone!" he commanded. "Go and stay with your mother, Woman Chief. You are a bad wife and not a very good mother. Stay away until you mend your ways."

Later that night when First Man was preparing food for his two young sons, his mother-in-law, Woman Chief, came to his hogan and scolded him for beating his wife. "Why do you men think you can treat us women in any manner you please?" asked Woman Chief. "It is we women who own our fields and work them. It is we women who prepare the meals and care for the children. Of what worth are you men, anyway?"

These words angered First Man greatly. Once he'd put his sons to bed he thought long and hard about the way his wife had been acting and the high handed manner in which Woman Chief had come into the hogan of her daughter to give orders. The more he thought about it, the more his anger grew until, at last he decided what he must do. The next morning he went about shouting for all the men to gather at the river but instructing the women to stay behind, "because I do not want to see them. I do not want to look upon the faces of those women." He sent someone to fetch his first born twins, the nadleeh, who were tending the common fields and irrigation system, "for they, too are men, although they know the ways of women."

At last the men all assembled at the river and First Man told them what had happened with his faithless wife and how his mother-in-law had treated him. "These women say they have no use of men," he said. "Let us men take the raft and go live on the other side of the river." Then he turned to the nadleeh twins, his first born. "What is it you have made for yourselves, my sons?" he asked.

"We have made cups and plates of all kinds and other utensils to use in the preparation of food. We have made wicker baskets which we have lined with pine pitch, hoes of the shoulder blades of deer we have made. Grinding stones, we each own. We have all these things we have thought of and made and taught the women to make," they replied.

"Go and bring all these things you have made without the help of any women. You will come across the river and live with us.

"We will leave now and live without the women. We will take those things we use with us and leave them behind with that thing they say makes a living for them. We will leave them over here with joosh and let them find out what a great hunter that is."

All day the nadleeh twins ferried men across the river on the raft of logs. Lastly they brought the young boys and the male infants, while the women kept the female children. When they got to the north side of the river Atse Hastiin sent the raft down to the Kisani for them to cross. They brought their women with them. However they traveled far down the river and to the east to live, as they were tiring of these quarrels among the new people.

Not all of the men were pleased to be parting from the women for many of them loved their wives and had not experienced the trouble First Man had. As soon as they had crossed the river the men immediately began working, but those who loved their wives and especially the young men did so with tears in their eyes. None of the men could return again once they reached the far shore because Tieholtsodi, glad the men had parted from the women, used his powers to stir the waters of the river constantly. He would allow only the nadleeh to cross back and forth.

Some of the men went out hunting right away—for the young boys needed food—while others set to work chopping down willows and building huts. By the end of four days they had shelters in which to live. It is told that they were happy at first, without women constantly telling them what to do and having the old mothers of their wives ordering them about.

That winter the women had an abundance of food, and they feasted, sang and had a good time. Often they came down to the edge of the river and called across to taunt the men, exposing themselves and asking them if they desired what they were missing. In the months following the separation they brought the newly born male children to the water's edge and the nadleeh crossed on the raft to bring them back to the men's side of the river.

The next year the men prepared a few small fields and raised some corn, but they did not have enough corn to eat and still had to live mostly by hunting. The women planted all of the old farm, but they did not work it very well and when the second winter came they had much less and did not sing and make merry as they had done the first year. In the second spring the women planted even less, while the men increased the size of their fields by clearing more land and planting more. Each year the fields and crops of the men increased, while those of the women diminished and they began to suffer for want of food. In the autumn of the third year of the separation many women jumped into the river and tried to swim over. But because the river reflected the turmoil of The People they were pulled under the current of the magical waters and never seen again. In the fourth year the men had more than they could eat; corn and pumpkins lay untouched in the fields, while the women were starving. Soon, those that were weak or old began dying.

At length, First Man began to think what the effect of his course might be. He realized that if he continued to keep the men and the women apart the race would die out, so he called the men together and spoke his thoughts to them. Some said, "Surely our race will perish," and others said, "What good is our abundance to us? We think so much of our poor women starving in our sight that we cannot eat."

First Man then sent one of the men to the river bank to call across to find if First Woman was still there, and to bid her come down to the river. She came to the bank, and First Man called to her and asked if she still thought she could live alone.

"No," she replied. "We cannot live without our husbands."

The women were then told to assemble at the shores of the stream. The raft was sent over and the women were ferried across. But before the women were allowed to mingle with the men they were made to bathe their bodies and dry them with corn meal as they were filthy and ragged and a disagreeable odor like that of coyote urine came from them. They were put into a corral and kept there four days before they were let out to join the men in their feasts.

Now during the separation, both men and women longed for each other and relieved their desires by practicing masturbation. The women satisfied themselves through intercourse with bones and horns, stones and cactus and with Coyote, who had remained with the women, it is said by some, to take advantage of the situation.

It is known that the men relieved themselves in a similar way.

One day, after a long hunt, a young man called Man With Wrappings On, managed to kill a deer. After removing the entrails of the beast, he thought he would satisfy his hunger by cooking the liver of the deer. But as he stared into the fire and held the liver in his hand he began to think on the women across the river. Using the liver, he started to relieve his sexual desires with it. Just as he did this, Neeshjaa, the Owl cried out, "Stop what you're doing! It is wrong."

Man With Wrappings On then started to put the liver back into the fire, but decided not to heed the words of the wise Owl. Again Neeshjaa said, "Stop that now, grandson, you know it is wrong. This will not help to continue the growth of The People."

This continued at length until the young man heeded the Owl's warnings.

Returning to the camp of the men, Man With Wrappings On told First Man what had happened, and how he desperately missed the women. Aste Hastiin who, after thinking about it saw the wisdom in the advice of Owl, agreed that the situation had gone bad for them. However, he first devised a test to put the men and women to before allowing them come together again. Once they were all bathed and blessed by corn meal, he lined up the naked women to the south and the naked men to the north, facing each other. The test was to see which desired to be reunited most. The men proved to be the weaker and gave in first.

And so until this day, it is the man who desires marriage more. However, since all this came about in part because Woman Chief interfered in the business of her son-in-law, it became the custom among the Navajo for women to avoid the presence of their sons-in-law and to visit their daughter only when they are certain that her husband is away from the home.

Through the transgressions of the women the Naye'i (alien gods or monsters) who afterwards nearly annihilated the human race, came into existence, but no evil consequences followed the transgressions of the men.

THE FIFTH WORLD

Together, The Lower Worlds Story, the tale of The Separation and the one that follows, The Emergence, make up the "stalk" of Navajo religion off which almost all other ceremonies branch. It is what Father Berard Haile, OFM, referred to as the "Upward Moving and Emergence Way." A detailed and elaborate explanation, for those who are interested in more than my cursory telling here, is the subject of the book of the same name with an excellent (as usual) introduction by Karl W. Lucket, published by the University of Nebraska Press. It includes a drawing, based on Father Haile's original, which was done on newsprint, showing the "Upward Moving Way" or haneelneehee, as a cornstalk off which all the important ceremonials branch. There are dozens of them, the major ones lasting from four to nine days. Several of the ceremonies, as collected by Father Haile, have been published in the American Tribal Religions series, with Karl Luckert as general editor.

I've found Navajo mythological tales to be amazingly consistent, considering the remoteness of the Navajoland

until recent times and that all of the people who recorded them were white and many came with their own
preconceived ideas and prejudices. Versions of the all-
important Tale of the Emergence, the journey through the
first four worlds and entry into the fifth world and the first
few decades of "earth surface" life may differ in particulars
from one version to another but basically the tales remain
pretty much the same. With a couple notable exceptions,
the tales don't really differ that much from one era to
another and as told by a Singer at Lupton, in the
southeastern part of the reservation, from a version told
years before at, say, Navajo Mountain, far to the north.
In comparing the work of Washington Matthews, who did
his field work not long after the Civil War, with that of
Father Haile, who began working on the reservation a
decade or so later, one might, at first, suspect little relationship in their versions of the same story.

The difference is, eventually, the sometimes formidable
detail found in the Haile version. It was only recently that
I made the time to actually study the published versions
of Navajo ceremonial tales as recorded by Haile in
detail—as opposed to the quick reading of them I'd done
before—and belatedly appreciate the work done by both
Haile and Karl Luckert, who notes in his introduction to
"Upward Moving and Emergence Way" that a Mary
Wheelright publication based on the same original
manuscript that came into his hand "significantly
departed" from the original. I have never seen the
Wheelwright version but Luckert's statement certainly
brought back to memory an observation I'd made several
years ago when I came upon a version of The Emergence
Story in the rare book section of a store in Gallup. The
book, long out of print, was *Navajo Creation Myth* as told
by Hasteen Klah and recorded by Mary C. Wheelwright.

It significantly departs from any other version of the story with which I'm familiar.

The book was published in 1942 by the Museum of Navajo Ceremonial Art (now the Wheelwright Museum) and is the one that has the blued-eyed, white skinned Christ-like "Begochiddy" in a flurry of mountain building, people-creating and law making in the Third World and, relating to the story that follows, leading his people up to the Fourth World in a manner reminiscent of the Biblical Moses leading the Jews out of Egypt.

Upon finding the rare copy of the book in Gallup in August of 1982 I discussed it with Ruth Green. Of course we both already knew that often non-Navajo recorders sometimes interject their own religious beliefs when writing the mythological tales. The temptation for some to try to make the tales fit somehow within the framework of Biblical stories seems to be just too great to resist.

At any rate the Wheelwright-Klah work contains elements not found anywhere else that I know of and yet the departure from the usual tellings are not so drastic that the overall work is suspect. In most of the other versions, while varying in particulars, the reason for expulsion from the Lower Worlds in sexual misconduct. Probably Wheelwright had problems dealing with that. It seems that Father Berard Haile, a Catholic priest, also had a few problems within that area. It doesn't make their work any less valuable, however the reader should be aware that some versions of the myths have been censored. For that matter, I've cleaned up a couple in this book by omitting some particulars that are not all that important and which more sensitive readers might find a bit unnerving.

Mary Wheelwright was a very well-heeled and well-intended lady from New England who spent a great deal of time and money in Navajoland collecting Navajo

Ceremonies and the accompanying "myths." Wheelright's work and that of Washington Matthews and certainly Father Berard Haile, is the barometer by which those of us who came along later should measure ourselves. Based on my own experience, I've always been amazed that they were able to accomplish as much as they did.

Wheelwright's contribution was invaluable and without her work, the wealth of material collected by the museum she founded in Santa Fe would not exist. And certainly Old Hastiin Klah earned his high esteem as one of the leading Singers of his day. He "owned" several ceremonies and was sought to conduct sings throughout Dinehtah.

He sometimes shocked his own people by revealing the mysteries of Navajo creation to the Bilagaana woman and others. He shocked them even more when he became the first to reproduce sandpaintings in yarn and weave Yei (holy figures) in a blanket. I have known one Singer who, as a young man, knew Klah, and the son of still another Singer who has some wonderful tales to tell about the "Old Medicine Man" as he sometimes referred to himself in jest, I'm told. In his version, either Klah or Wheelwright, as mentioned earlier, has the deity Begochidi in a flurry of creating in the Lower Worlds that is, in all other versions I know off, done by others, mostly by First Man. And Begochidi is described as "the blue-eyed and yellow-haired god, the great god (of all)." Klah's version shows attrition to Christian influence either because he, himself, had been overly influenced by the missionaries who were very active in the Newcomb area where he lived all of his life or he was sensitive to the beliefs of Wheelright, his benefactor. Gladys Reichard (1944, p. 19) suggests that Mary Wheelwright, herself, might have been responsible for the "Christization" of the Klah version of The

Emergence Story . . .

There is still another possibility, however remote in this instance. It is the custom of Navajo Singers to make some slight changes or leave out portions of a tale being told to an outsider. Perhaps Hasteen Klah did just that. Or, since he was said to possess a keen sense of humor, maybe the blaze of creation amid colors of the rainbow by Begochidi in his version was nothing more than a little funning at the expense of Wheelright on the part of "the Old Medicine Man" in the early days of their relationship when she recorded his version of the Navajo Creation Myth. Whatever, the Klah version pretty much coincides with others once the beings reach the Fifth World of the Navajo cosmos.

THE EMERGENCE STORY

When the women were let out of the corral that first night following the Separation of the Sexes, it was found that three of them were missing. After dark, voices were heard calling from the other side of the river. They were the voices of the missing ones—a mother and her two daughters. They begged to be ferried over, but the men told them it was too dark, that they must wait until morning. Upon hearing this reply, they jumped into the river and tried to swim across. The mother succeeded in reaching the opposite bank and finding her husband. The daughters were seized by Tieholtsodi, the water monster, and dragged down under the water.

For three days and three nights nothing was heard of the young women and The People supposed them lost forever. But on the morning of the fourth day the call of the gods was heard—four times as usual—and after the fourth call White Body made his appearance, holding up two fingers and pointing at the river. The People supposed that these signs had reference to the lost girls. Some of the men crossed the stream on the raft and found the tracks of the lost ones, which they traced to the edge of the water. White Body went away, but soon returned, accompanied by Blue Body. White Body carried a large bowl of white shell, and Blue Body a large bowl of blue shell. They asked for a man and a woman to accompany them, and they went down to the river. They put both the bowls on the surface of the water and caused them to spin around. Beneath the spinning bowls the water opened, for it was hollow, and gave entrance to a large house of four rooms.

The man and the woman descended and Coyote, ever curious and meddling, followed them. In the room to the east, which was made of light-colored waters, they found nothing. In the room that was to the south, which was made of blue waters, they they again found nothing. And in the room in the west, which was made of yellow waters, they found that it contained nothing. But when they went into the room in the north, which was made of waters of all colors, they found the water monster Tieholtsodi, with the two girls he had stolen, and two children of his own. The man and the woman demanded the return of the stolen girls, and as he said nothing in reply, they took them and walked away. But as they went out, Coyote, unperceived by all, took the two children of Tieholtsodi and carried them off under his robe. Now Coyote always wore his robe folded close around his body and always slept with it folded in this manner, so no one was surprised to see that he still wore his robe in this way when he came up from the waters of the river—and of course no one suspected that he had stolen the children of Tieholtsodi.

The next day the people were surprised to see deer, turkey, and antelope running past from east to west, and to see animals of six different kinds (two kinds of Hawks, two kinds of Squirrels, the Hummingbird, and the Bat) come into the camp seeking refuge. The concern of the people grew as the game animals ran past in increasing numbers for three days. On the morning of the fourth day, when the white light rose, The People observed in the east a strange white gleam along the horizon, and they sent out the Locust couriers to see what caused this unusual white light. The Locust returned at sunset and told the people that a vast flood of waters was fast approaching from the east. On hearing this, the people all assembled together, theKisani along with the others, in a great multitude, and they wailed and pulled at their hair over the approaching catastrophe. The people wept and moaned all night. The next morning, when the white light arose in the east, the waters were seen high as mountains encircling the whole horizon, except in the west, and rolling on rapidly. The people packed up all their goods as fast as they could, and ran up on a high hill nearby, for temporary safety. Here they held a council. Some one suggested that perhaps the two Squirrels (Hazaitso and Hazai) might help them.

"We will see what we can do," said the Squirrels. One planted a pinon see, the other a juniper seed, and they grew very rapidly. The people hoped that they would soon grow so tall that the flood could not reach their tops and that they all might find shelter there. But after the trees had grown to normal size they began to branch out and grew no higher. Then The people, more frightened than ever, called on the Weasels (Dlu'ilgai and Dlu'ilitso) for help. One of these planted a spruce seed and the other a pine seed. The trees sprouted at once and grew fast, and the people began to hope they would be saved from the flood that was surely coming. However, soon the trees began to branch and eventually they dwindled to slender points at the top and ceased to grow higher. Now the people were in the depths of despair, for the waters were coming nearer with each moment. It was then that they saw two men approaching the hill on which they were gathered. One of the men was very old and gray of hair while the other, who walked in advance, was young, strong and handsome. They ascended the hill and passed through the crowd, speaking to no one. The young man sat down on the summit, the old man sat down behind him, and Locust sat down behind the old man—all facing east.

The old man took seven bags from beneath his robe and opened them. Each contained a small quantity of earth. He told The People that the earth was from the seven sacred mountains. (There were in the Fourth World seven sacred mountains, named and placed the same as the sacred mountains of the present Navajoland).

"Ah, perhaps our father can do something for us," said the people.

"I cannot, but my son may be able to help you," suggested the old man.

Then they begged the son to help them and he said that he would if they would all move away from where he stood, face to the west and not look around until he called them; for no one should see him at his work. They did as he asked and in a few moments he called and told them to come to him. When they came they saw that he had spread the sacred earth on the ground and planted thirty-two reeds in it, each of which had thirty-two joints. As they watched they saw the roots of the reeds striking out into the soil and growing rapidly downward. A moment later all the reeds joined together and became one reed of great size, with a hole in its eastern side. The young man then told them to enter the hollow of the reed through this hole. When they were all safely inside, the opening closed. Scarcely had it closed when they heard the loud noise of the waters surging outside.

The waters rose fast but the reed grew faster, and soon it grew so high that it began to sway. The people inside, of course, were in great fear that their weight would cause the reed to break and topple over into the water. White Body, Blue Body, Yellow Body and Black Body were along. Black Body blew a great breath out through a hole in the top of the reed; a heavy dark cloud formed around the reed and kept it steady. But as the reed grew higher and higher, it again began to sway, and again The people within were in great fear, whereupon Black Body blew and made another cloud to steady the reed.

By the time darkness fell the great reed had grown up close to the sky, but it swayed and waved so much that they could not secure it until Black Body, who was up-permost, took the plume out of his headband and stuck it out through the top of the cane against the sky to secure it, and this is why the reed (Phragmites communis) always carries a plume on its head now.

Still the water continued to rise. As the Turkey was the last to enter the reed, he was at the bottom. When the waters rose high enough to wet the Turkey he began to gobble and the people knew that danger was near. Often did the waves wash the end of the Turkey's tail and it is for this reason that the tips of the turkey's tail feathers are, to this day, lighter in color than the rest of his plumage.

Seeing no hole in the sky, The People sent up the Great Hawk, to see what he could do. He flew up and began to scratch at the sky with his claws, and he scratched and scratched until he was lost to sight. After a while he came back and said that he had scratched to where he could see light, but he could not get through the sky. Next they sent up all the digging animals, each in turn, to try to dig through the sky to the Fifth World. The Bear tried first and he grew tired, then the Wolf, the Coyote and the Lynx, each trying to dig through and each growing tired in turn. The Badger was the last to try and while he was digging, water began to drip down from above. The people knew they had struck the waters of the upper world but the Badger was too tired to dig any more. Next Locust was sent up. He made a shaft in the soft mud, such as locusts make to this day, and managed to reach this, the Fifth World.

Locust was gone a long time and when he returned he had this story to tell: He had gotten through to the upper world and came out on a little island in the center of a lake. When he got out he was approached from the east by a White Grebe (Swan in other versions), from the south by a Blue Grebe, from the west by a Yellow Grebe and from the north by a Black Grebe. The Grebes told the Locust that they owned this upper world and offered him a challenge. "If you can do as we do," they said, "we shall give you this world. If you cannot, you must die."

Each of the Grebes had an arrow made of the black wind. Each in turn passed the arrow from side to side through his heart and flung it down to Wonistisidi, the Locust. The Locust picked up the arrows and ran them from side to side through his heart as he had seen the Grebes do, and threw them down. The Grebes departed, leaving the land to the Locust. To this day we see in every Locust'a sides the holes made by the arrows.

But the hole the Locust made in ascending to the Fifth World was too small for many of the people, so they sent

Badger up to make it larger. When Badger came back his legs were stained black with mud, and the legs of all badgers have been black ever since. Then First Man and First Woman led the way and all the others followed them, and climbed up through the hole to the surface of this—the Fifth World.

They came out into this Fifth World on an island in the middle of lake. This lake in which they emerged was surrounded by high cliffs, from the top of which stretched a great plain. Finding no way out of the lake, they called on Blue Body to help them. Blue Body had brought four stones with him from the lower world, and he threw one of each toward the four cardinal points against the cliffs, breaking holes through the cliffs through which the waters flowed away in four directions. While the lake did not altogether drain out through the holes Blue Body had made, the bottom did become bare in one place—in the east—connecting the island with the mainland. But the mud was so deep in this place that the people still hesitated to cross so they prayed to Smooth Wind to come to their aid. The wind came and in one day dried up the mud so that the people could easily walk over. While they were waiting for the ground to dry, the Kisani camped on the east side of the island and built a wall of mud and stone to shelter them from the wind, and the Navajo built a shelter of brushwood for protection against the wind. That is why the Pueblos build houses of stone and adobe now and the Navajo build brushwood shelters for protection against the summer wind. And that is why the true Pueblos live in lands to the east.

The next day, when they reached the mainland, they sought to divine their fate. To do this one of the people threw a hide-scraper into the water, saying :"If it sinks we perish, if it floats we live." It floated and all rejoiced.

But Coyote said, "Let me divine your fate." He picked up a stone and said, "If it sinks we perish, if it floats we live, " as he threw it into the water. The stone sank and all the people were angry with him, but he answered them saying, "If we all live, and continue to increase as we have done, the earth will soon become too small to hold all of us, and there will be no more room for cornfields. It is better that each of us should live but a time on this earth and then leave and make room for our children." The People saw the wisdom of his words and were silent.

On the fourth day after the emergence someone went to look at the hole through which they had come from the underworld and saw water welling up there; already it was nearly to the top of the hole and each moment it grew higher. Quickly he ran back to his people and told them what he had seen. A council was called at once to consider the new danger that threatened them. First Man, who rose to speak, stared at Coyote who had pointed knowingly with his protruded lips at the rising water. "Yonder is a rascal, that Coyote, and there is something wrong about him. He never takes off his robe, even when he lies down to sleep. I have watched him for a long time, and have suspected that he carries some stolen property under his robe. Let us search him."

They tore the robe from Coyote's shoulders and two strange little objects that resembled buffalo calves, but were spotted all over in various colors, dropped out. These were the children of Tieholtsodi. At once the people threw them into the hole through wihich the waters were pouring and in an instant the waters subsided and rushed back into the lower world with a deafening noise. Once Tieholtsodi had found his children, he was no longer interested in those who had escaped to the Earth Surface. He had caused the flood so that he might search the water for his children which Coyote had stolen.

On the fifth night after arriving in the Fifth World, one of the twin Nadleeh ceased to breathe. They left him alone all that night and, when morning came, Coyote proposed to lay him at rest among the rocks. This they did, but they all wondered what had become of his breath. They went in various directions to seek its trail, but could find it nowhere. While they were hunting, two men went over to the hole from which they had emerged from the lower world. It occurred to one of them to look down into the hole. He did so, and saw the dead one seated by the side of the river in the Fourth World, combing his hair. Then he returned to the people and told them what he had seen, but in four days he died. Ever since the Navajos have feared to look upon the dead or to behold a ghost, lest they die themselves.

Soon after this it was learned that the Kisani, who had made their camp a little distance away from the others, had brought an ear of corn for seed form the lower world. Some of the people proposed that they go to the camp of the Kisani and take the corn away from them. But others, of better counsel, said that this would be wrong as the Pueblos had suffered as much as the rest, and if they had the foresight to bring corn with them from the lower world they should profit by it. In spite of these words, some of the young men went to the Kisani and demanded the corn.

After some angry talk on both sides, the Kisani said, "We will break the ear in two and give you whichever half you choose." The young men agreed to this proposition and the woman who owned the ear of corn broke it in the middle and laid the pieces down for the others to choose. The young men looked at the pieces considering which they should choose, when Coyote impatiently picked up the tip end of the ear and made off with it. The Kisani kept the butt, and this is the reason the Pueblos have always had better crops than the Navajos. But the Pueblos had become alarmed at the threats and angry language of their neighbors and moved away from them to the east, and this is why the Navajos and the Pueblos now live apart from one another.

After the Kisani had moved away, First Man and First Woman, Black Body and Blue Body left the people and set out to build the seven sacred mountains of the present Navajo land. They made them all of earth which they had brought from similar mountains in the Fourth World. The mountains they made were Tsisnaajini in the East, Tsoodzil in the South, Doko'oosliid in the West and Dibentsaa in the North. They also made Ch'oolii, Dzil'na'oodilii, and Naatsis'aan in the middle of the land.

Through Tsisnaajini (Mount Blanca) in the east, they ran a bolt of lightning to fasten it to earth and decorated it with white shells, white lightning, white corn, dark clouds and male rain. (The Navajos refer to a heavy downpour as a "male rain.") Then they set a large bowl of shell on its summit in which they placed two eggs of the pigeon to make feathers for the mountain. They covered the eggs with a sacred buckskin to make them hatch and all these things they covered with a sheet of daylight. Then they put Rock Crystal Boy and Rock Crystal Girl, the deities of Tsisnaajini, into the mountain to dwell. The deities were brought up from the lower world as small pieces of clear quartz, but as soon as they were placed in the mountain they came to life.

Next they made the sacred mountain of the south, Tsoodzil, (Mount Taylor), and fastened it to the Earth with a great stone knife, thrust through from top to bottom. They adorned Tsoodzil with turquoise, with dark mist, female rain and different kinds of game animals. On its summit they placed a dish of turquoise in which they put two eggs of the bluebird, which they covered with the sacred buckskin to make them hatch, and over all these things they spread a covering of blue sky. Into this mountain to dwell they placed the Boy Who Carries One Turquoise and the Girl Who Carries One Grain of Corn.

They fastened Doko'oosliid (San Francisco Peaks), the sacred mountain of the west, to the earth with a sunbeam and adorned it with haliotis shell, with black clouds, male rain, yellow corn and all sorts of wild animals. Upon the top of Doko'oosliid they placed a dish made of haliotis shell and placed in it two eggs of the yellow warbler, covering them with the sacred buckskin. Over all this they spread a yellow cloud and placed White Corn Boy and Yellow Corn Girl to dwell.

They fastened Dibentsaa (Mount Hesperus), the sacred mountain of the North, to the earth with a rainbow and adorned it with black beads, dark mist, with many kinds of plants and many different wild animals. On its top they placed a dish of paszini (black beads) in which they placed two eggs of the blackbird, over which they laid a sacred buckskin. Over all this they spread a covering of darkness. Then they put Pollen Boy and Grasshopper Girl in the mountain to dwell.

Ch'oolii was fastened to the earth with a cord of rain. They decorated it with pollen, the dark mist and female rain. On top of Tsolihi they placed a yellow bird called tsozgali (species undetermined), and they put Boy Who Produces Jewels and Girl Who Produces Jewels in the mountain to live.

They fastened the mountain of Naatsis'aan to the earth with a mirage stone (silicate of magnesia) and decorated it with black clouds, male rain and all sorts of beautiful plates. They placed a live grasshopper to live on its summit and inside they put Mirage Stone Boy and Carnelian Girl to dwell.

Now as The People only had three lights and the darkness from the lower worlds in the Fifth World, First Man and First Woman thought they might form some lights which would make the world brighter. After much discussion, they decided to make the Sun and Moon. For the sun they made a round flat object, like a dish, out of a clear stone. They set turquoises around the edge and around the edge and outside of these they put rays of red rain, lightning and snakes of many kinds. For a while they debated putting four points on it, as they afterwards did to the stars, but finally they decided to leave it round. They made the Moon of crystal and bordered it with white shells. Upon its face they put sheet lightning and all kinds of water.

Then they held a council to decide what to do with the Sun and the Moon. The East Wind begged that they might belong to his land, so the people dragged them off to the edge of the world where he dwelt. There they gave the Sun to the young man who had planted the great reed in the lower world and appointed him to carry it. To his father, the old gray-haired man, they gave the Moon to carry. These men had had no names before this, but now the young man was given the name of Tsohanoai, and the old one was named Klehanoai. When they were about to depart, in order to begin their labors, a great sorrow came upon the people, for they were loved by all. But First Man said, "Mourn not for them, for you will see them in the heavens."

On the fifth day after The People entered the Fifth World, the Sun climbed to the zenith and stopped. The day grew hot and The People all longed for the night to come but the Sun did not move. Then the Coyote, who had invented death by tossing a stone in the water, said: "The Sun has stopped because he has not been paid for his work. He demands a human life for every day that he labors and he will not move again until someone dies."

Soon a woman, the wife of a great chief, ceased to breathe and grew cold, and while they all drew around her in wonder, the Sun was observed to move again, and he travelled down the sky and passed behind the western mountains. That night the Moon stopped in the zenith, as the Sun had done during the day, and the Coyote told The People that the Moon also demanded payment and would not move until it was given. He had scarcely spoken when the man who had seen the departed Nadleeh in the lower world died and the Moon, satisfied, continued his journey to the west. And thus it is that someone must die each day and each night or the Sun and the Moon would not continue to journey across the sky. And that was what First Man meant when he told the people not to mourn for the old man and his son, for all that die will join them in the heavens and become theirs in return for their labors.

THE CREATION OF THE SACRED MOUNTAINS
THE LIGHT, AND HORSES
OF THE FIFTH WORLD

O ld Navajo men like to tell the story and I've heard it several times. I've also heard from young Navajo women, for that matter. When the Spaniards first came up from Mexico in the sixteenth century, it is said the Navajos looked upon them from afar and said: "Oh, look! Those Mexicans have brought our horses back to us."

In 1936, archaeologists discovered evidence of an early man in a cave in the Sandia Mountain range east of Albuquerque. Bone left besides campfires indicate people of the Sandia culture were hunting horses twenty-five hundred years before the Spaniards reintroduced a later version of that animal to New Mexico. Actually, ancestors of Equus, the modern horse, originated in North America during the Pliocene era, and subsequently migrated to South America and the Old World. It seems that the horse, the three-toed original (about the size of a dog) and a later, the one-toed or hooved ancestor of the present-day horse were both native to North America and had, for whatever reason, died out (or was hunted to extinction by those First Americans as has been suggested by some scholars) before the Spanish reintroduced them.

The Arabian horses the Spaniards brought with them to the Americas were descended from animals brought across the Strait of Gibraltar by the Moors when they invaded the Iberian Peninsula in AD 711.

There is no way of knowing exactly when the ancestors of the Navajo acquired the horse. In February of 1540, Francisco Vasquez de Coronado left Mexico City for the north, set on plundering the fabled "Seven Golden Cities of Cibola" of Spanish folklore. Over three hundred Spanish foot soldiers led an Indian force of eight hundred men; there were five hundred war horses, adorned with their own coats of mail, bearing armored cavalry, followed by almost a thousand work horses and mules hauling munitions and provisions, and bringing up the rear were hundreds of sheep and cattle for food. Many of the soldiers brought along their wives and children, ready-made colonists to hold the land once "Cibola" had been defeated.

Two years later, in the summer of 1542, less than a hundred members of the expedition straggled back to Mexico, a ragged, disgraced band. In searching for the "true Cibola" Coronado found New Mexico adobe villages that were most definitely not covered with "gold and precious stones" as he'd been led to believe. He also found Pueblo, Apache and other war chiefs who were willing to fight to the death at every stop, and who were clever enough to send him on a fool's errand looking for Cibola through the empty plains of what is now Texas and as far north as Kansas.

The impact the Coronado expedition made on the Pueblos, Apaches and Navajos of New Mexcio was deep and lasting. Not only were there strange men in the land but there were also sheep and cattle. And horses. Indeed, these strange men dressed in metal came to be, in Nava-

jo, the people which Kelhanoai, the Moon Bearer, had
made and given to the divine gambler, Nohoilpi (the story
follows this one), to punish the Dineh for the way they'd
treated him!

There were five more expeditions made into New Mexico by the Spanish over the next fifty years, all, of course,
with horses. Then, in 1598, Jaun de Onate brought 400
soldiers and colonists along with a thousand head of stock,
including horses, cattle, sheep, hog, mules and jackasses.
Taking possession of the "newly discovered land" Onate
set up a temporary capitol at the Tewa pueblo of Ohke,
where the Chama enters the Rio Grande. In 1610 Santa
Fe was founded and sometime during this period the Navajos started helping themselves to Spanish horses and sheep.
Their horses had returned, they said.

Certainly, it is hard to believe that the horse existed in
Navajo tribal memory over all those centuries. However,
the creation of the horse by their gods is an integral chapter
in the story of Creation and Emergence. And certainly that
epic mythology has existed in the Southwest longer than
the modern horses introduced by the Spaniards.

At any rate, the Navajos have their own version of how
this wonderful beast they'd come to love so much was
created for them by the gods.

All cultures who became great horsemen have a myth
of how this extraordinary animal was created. The ancient
Greeks gave the God of the Sea, Poseidon, credit for
creating the horse as well as the Centuar, the half-man,
half-horse creature who came thundering from the sea to
plunder and lustfully kidnap women. Of course the Aztecs
also thought man and horse was one animal when they
first encountered mounted Spanish Conquistadores. By the
time they realized their mistake, the Spaniards had rallied
their over-taxed subject nations who were in revolt in any

case. It merely took a couple hundred mounted Conquistadores riding ahead of a couple hundred thousand
Indians in revolt to rout the mighty Aztecs.

The Arabs, along with the Navajo the greatest horsemen
in the world, it has been said, had their own version of
a divine creation of the horse.

The story of the creation of the sun, moon, stars and
sacred mountains is told in a brief version at the end of
the Emergence Story which precedes this one. That version is one I collected in the early 1970s and follows
Matthews.

As I've stated, Navajo myth tales sometimes differ but
almost always only slightly. Here, the creation of the horse
by Begochidi, youngest son of the Sun Bearer, is preced-
ed by a slightly different version of the creation of the sun,
moon, stars and sacred mountains than the one that ap-
pears at the end of the Emergence Story. It was collected
in 1982 and is a bit richer in detail and tells more about
First Man and First Woman and how they behaved once
they entered the Fifth World.

THE CREATION
OF THE SACRED MOUNTAINS

Just as had happened in the Fourth World, the Kisani
decided it was not worth the bother of living with these
quarrelsome people and moved away, going to the south
and east and that is why the Navajos and the Pueblos have
always lived apart since.

It was then that First Man and First Woman, Black Body
and Blue Body put their heads together and decided they'd
best get on with building the sacred mountains such as
they had had in the Fourth World. First Man had brought

some dirt from each of the mountains up through the reed with him for that purpose. They set out there from the Place of Emergence (located in southwestern Colorado, near Hesperus Peak), to get on about the business of building in order that the people could properly do the ceremonials the gods had taught them. Then it was like today, and the ceremonials should only be done as prescribed and within the bounds of the four cardinal sacred mountains.

So, they left the people and set out to build the seven sacred mountains of the present Navajo land. They made them all of materials which they had brought from the similar mountains in the Fourth World. The mountains they made were Tsisnaajini in the East, Tsoodzil in the South, Doko'oosliid in the West and Dibentsaa in the North. They also made Ch'oolii, Dzil'na'oodilii, and Naatsis'aan in the middle of the land.

"Where shall we put these mountains?" First Man asked.

"We will place them as they were placed in the world below," First Woman answered. Then, turning to the east she threw a white stone she had taken from the Sacred Mountain of the East in the Fourth World. "There," she said. "Where that stone has landed we will put Tsisnaajini." They traveled for several days and found the stone.

Through Tsisnaajini (Mount Blanca) in the East, they ran a bolt of lightning to fasten it to earth and decorated it with white shells, white lightning, white corn, dark clouds and male rain. (The Navajos refer to a heavy downpour as a "male rain.") Then they set a large bowl of shell on its summit in which they placed two eggs of the Gray Dove (Hasbidi) to make feathers for the mountain. They covered the eggs with a sacred buckskin to make them hatch and all these things they covered with a sheet of daylight. Then they put Rock Crystal Boy and Rock Crystal Girl, the male and female gods of Tsisnaajini, into the mountain to dwell.

The deities were brought up from the lower world as small images of crystal, but as soon as they were placed in the mountain they came to life.

Once again they followed the stone, a turquoise, which First Woman had thrown. It was also sacred, having been brought up from the Fourth World.

They arrived to where the turquoise had made a dent in the earth and there they made the sacred mountain of the south, Tsoodzil, (Mount Taylor), and fastened it to the Earth with a great stone knife, thrust through from top to bottom. They adorned Tsoodzil with turquoise, with dark mist, female rain and different kinds of game animals. On its summit they placed a dish of turquoise in which they put two eggs of the Bluebird, which they covered with the sacred buckskin to make them hatch, and over all these things they spread a covering of blue sky. Into this mountain to dwell they placed the Boy Who Carries One Turquoise and the Girl Who Carries One Grain of Corn.

Again they followed a sacred stone thrown by First Woman, this time a piece of agate. It was to the west they journeyed now.

They fastened Doko'oosliid (San Francisco Peaks), the sacred mountain of the West, to the earth with a sunbeam and adorned it with haliotis shell, with black clouds, male rain, yellow corn and all sorts of wild animals. Upon the top of Doko'oosliid they placed a dish made of haliotis shell and placed in it two eggs of the Yellow Warbler, covering them with the sacred buckskin. Over all this they spread a yellow cloud and placed White Corn Boy and Yellow Corn Girl to dwell.

That done, First Woman took from the pocket of her garment a piece of jet and threw it to the north. It landed not too far from the Place of Emergence and near where the people were then living.

They fastened Dibentsaa (Mount Hesperus), the sacred mountain of the North, to the earth with a rainbow and adorned it with black beads, dark mist, with many kinds of plants and many different wild animals. On its top they placed a dish of paszini (black beads) in which they placed two eggs of the Blackbird, which they covered with a sacred buckskin. Over all this they spread a covering of darkness. Then they put Pollen Boy and Grasshopper Girl in the mountain to dwell.

Dzil Na'oodilli (Huerfano Mountain in northern New Mexcio), they fastened to the earth with a sunbeam. They decorated it with all kinds of things, including the dark clouds that make the male rain. They put nothing on the top, for they wished to keep it empty so that in the future warriors might be able to fight there. They placed Boy Who Produces Goods there and Girl Who Produces Goods there to dwell forever as gods.

Ch'oolii (Gobernador Knob in northern New Mexico) was fastened to the earth with a cord of rain. They decorated it with pollen, the dark mist and female rain. On top of Ch'oolii they placed a yellow bird called Tsozgali (Bullock Oriole) and they put Boy Who Produces Jewels and Girl Who Produces Jewels in the mountain to live.

They fastened the mountain of Naatsis'aan (Spruce Mountain, also in old Dine Bah, in northern New Mexcio) to the earth with a mirage stone (silicate of magnesia) and decorated it with black clouds, male rain and all sorts of plants. They placed a live Grasshopper to live on its summit and inside they put Mirage Stone Boy and Carnelian Girl to dwell.

Done with building the scared mountains of the Fifth World, First Man, First Woman, Blue Body and Black Body returned to where the people were living.

CREATION
OF THE SUN, MOON AND STARS

Now as The People only had three lights and the darkness from the lower worlds in the Fifth World, First Man and First Woman thought they might form some lights in the sky which would make the world brighter. After much discussion, they decided to make the Sun and Moon. So Atse Hastiin collected the people together and they brought with them all the things to make the Sun: white and yellow pollen, rainbows, rays and turquoise. The same ingredients were used to make the lesser of the luminaries, the moon.

For the sun they made a round flat object, like a dish, out of a clear stone. They set turquoises around the rim of the dish and around the edge and outside of these stones they put rays of red rain, sheet lightning and snakes of many kinds. Then they covered it with pollen, both white and yellow, and sang the proper songs. For a while they debated putting four points on it, as they afterwards did to the stars, but finally they decided to leave it round. They made the Moon of crystal and bordered it with white shells. Upon its face they put sheet lightning and all kinds of water, and covered it, too, with sacred pollen and sang the proper songs.

Next they held a council to decide what to do with the Sun and the Moon. For a while they considered putting them on top of Tsoodzil (Mount Taylor) and having them directed by the Spirit People as to when they should give off their light. Others, however, thought this over and said: "If we put them on the mountaintop how will all the world see the light?" Black Body saw the sense of this and pointed out that only those living near that place would be able to see them and therefore they'd do the rest of the people no good.

At long last, the East Wind begged that they might belong to his land, so the people dragged them off to the edge of the world where he dwelt. Still, the problem of how to get them into the sky and cause them to move around so the entire world might benefit from their light presented a problem. Thinking this over, First Man decided that a young man would carry the sun across the sky every day on his back. He gave the Sun to the young man who had planted the great reed in the lower world and appointed him to carry it. The young man said that he would accept the responsibility, but did not want to be separated from his beloved father.

"If that is your wish," said First Man, "then we will have your father carry the moon." And that is why the moon moves more slowly and less predictably than the sun.

To the father, the old gray haired man, he gave a rainbow so he might carry the moon; to the son he gave the same. These men had had no names before this, but now the young man was given the name of Tsohanoai (or Tsinhanoai) and the old one was named Klehanoai. When they were about to depart, in order to begin their labors, a great sorrow came upon the people, for they were loved by all. But First Man said, "Mourn not for them, for you will see them in the heavens."

Using rainbows, First Man placed the Bearer of the Sun and the Moon Carrier, along with the Sun's children into the sky to begin the task they had accepted.

For the first three days, the Sun used his time to make his hogan. Using poles of White Lightning, he fashioned the frame. Turquoise, jet, white shell, and abalone formed the four sides. It was a magnificent house made of the most precious things known to The People.

But all the while the Sun was making his house, The People grew nervous for the sun was not moving. It stayed directly overhead, while the Moon Carrier grew increasingly weak—moving slower and slower each day.

First Man grew impatient with the Sun Bearer and called to him saying: "You have promised to take the sun across the sky each day. Now it has been three days. Your father grows weak. I have many things to do for The People so you must carry out your task. In addition, I want you to create some of the earth animals that we did not have in our previous world." Three times he said this, and then the Sun responded: "Yes, father of all, I will do as you ask."

On the fifth day after The People entered the Fifth World, the Sun climbed to the zenith and stopped. The day grew hot and the people all longed for the night to come but the Sun did not move. Then Coyote, who had invented death by tossing a stone in the water, said: "The Sun has stopped because he has not been paid for his work. He demands a human life for every day that he labors and he will not move again until someone dies."

Soon a woman, the wife of wise and respected man, ceased to breathe and grew cold, and while they all drew around her in wonder, the Sun was observed to move again, and he travelled down the sky and passed behind the western mountains. That night the Moon stopped in the zenith, as the Sun had done during the day, and Coyote told the people that the Moon also demanded payment and would not move until it was given. He had scarcely spoken when the man who had seen the departed nadleeh in the lower world died and the Moon, satisfied, continued his journey to the West.

And thus it is that someone must die each day and each

night or the Sun and the Moon will not continue to journey across the sky. And that was what First Man meant when he told the people not to mourn for the old man and his son, for all that died will join them in the heavens and become theirs in return for their giving light to the earth.

After this First Man and First Woman, still not satisfied with the sky and the way it looked, began the task of making the stars. The Sun and Moon alone did not provide sufficient beauty. So, they searched for glittering stones and found some mica dust as well. First Man placed the Star Which Does Not Move at the pole of the heavens. Then he placed the seven stars (Ursa Major) to grow around it. Then he placed four bright stars at the four quarters of the sky, and designed the groups of stars around them. Next First Woman picked up three shining red pieces of stone and threw them up to become three red dwarf stars. And so, one by one the stars were placed in the sky and the constellations formed: Corvbus in the east, then Big Snake and Bear, Thunder and Scorpio and aside of Ursa Major they (First Man and First Woman) placed Cassiopoea, then Orion, Aldebaran in Taurus and so forth. Growing impatient with this orderly creation of the heavens, Coyote snatched up the bag containing the star materials and flung its contents across the sky, creating the Milky Way. "There, now," he said. "That looks better." But finding still another star in the bag, Coyote flung it off to the south where it remains in the sky and is called "Coyote's Star" by the Navajos. And this is where the stars remain today.

With the business of the scared mountains and the sky taken care of, First Man realized that there were other things that needed his attention. For one thing both Tsohanoai and Klehanaoai seem to need direction. Generally they arose off in the land of East Wind but sometimes grew confused as to which direction they should go. So First Man placed Dawn in the east, Skyblue in the south, Evening Twilight in the west and Darkness in the north as these things should be. Then he instructed Tsohanoai and Klehanoai to pay attention to these directions.

First Woman and Coyote had decided there should be seasons, a season for planting, one for growing, another for gathering and one for resting. There was some disagreement about how many months there should be in the seasons but finally it was decided that there would be twelve in all, six to the north—October, November, December, January, February and March—which would be winter months and belong to the sky, and six to to the south—April, May, June, July, August, and September, which would be the summer months and belong to the earth. The Navajos have other names for the months, of course, but just as the Bilaganna have, there are twelve months in the old Navajo way of counting the year.

THE CREATION OF THE HORSE

On the fourth day, the Bearer of the Sun collected all the remaining materials from the building of his house and decided to make something useful of these leftover goods.

Then he called out to the Spirit People to breathe life into these things. The first creature to rise out of the rubble was much like what we know today as a horse—and it came from the turquoise that was left from building the Sun's hogan.

The Sun, knowing his father often grew tired and needed help in carrying the moon across the sky, called out: "Father, could you use this creature of turquoise to carry you across the sky?"

His father examined the creature from afar and returned: "It looks much too heavy and slow; could there be another such creature?"

The Sun called out to the Spirit People and this time two creatures much like the one of turquoise rose from the jet and the white shell. The Sun then again called to his father: "Could you perhaps use one of these creatures I have created in order to more easily carry that moon across the sky?"

Again his father looked the creatures over and answered: "The one of jet would blanket out the light I have to carry, and the one of white shell is much too bright and looks too fast; is there anything else you have made that would be of use?"

The Sun looked down and all there was left was some abalone shell. Again, he called out to the Spirit People and a fourth creature much like a horse arose from the shell. He called a fourth time to his father: "Could you, my father, use this beast to help you in your task?"

And for the fourth time his father looked the newly made creature over. This time he took much longer. Finally he returned: "Yes, my son, this creature seems tame enough and is of the right color to make my responsibility much easier. I thank you." The Moon Carrier mounted the abalone creature and continued his path across the sky. And this is why the moon has much the same color as abalone.

By this time the Sun Bearer was getting tired himself—and he still had to carry the sun across the sky. He thought of what his father had said about the white shell creature, how it was much too bright and looked too fast. This was true in the case where the Moon Bearer was concerned, for he was old and slow and had little need for speed.

But for the Sun it would be the perfect creature to help him in his task of carrying the sun across the sky. So, he mounted the white shell beast, putting the sun disk under his right arm and continued his quest across the sky. He would give the turquoise creature to Changing Woman and the jet creature to his favorite son, Begochidi.

Tsohanoai was proud of what he had done for his father and himself as he rode across the sky. The Little Winds began to tell him certain things about the creatures he had created and the sun disk he carried across the sky. They told him: "The People will need creatures like the ones you and your father ride across the sky. Also, the sun disk you carry under your right arm is to be a sign for The People. When the Spirit People tell you to carry the sun under your left arm, it will go black—this is called an eclipse, and it will mean danger will soon be coming for The People." And with that, the Little Winds left him.

Feeling the importance of the message given to him, the Bearer of the Sun decided to go to the earth and tell The People of what he had learned. Riding down a rainbow, he switched the sun disk to his left side and the sky went dark. He called out to The People: "This is called an eclipse, and when this happens it is a message from the Spirit People that there is impending danger." And this is why the sun has eclipses.

When Tsohanoai returned to the House of the Sun, he began the immense task of creating the earth animals that First Man had instructed him to make. He made the antelope, the ground squirrels, the prairie dogs and many of the little birds that did not exist in the Fourth World. But as he did this, The Little Winds returned to him reminding him that The People needed a beast on the earth much like the creatures he had created for himself and his father.

Thinking on this, the Sun called to his youngest son and said: "Son, I am busy making the antelope and other creatures for the earth. You will have to make that creature the Little Winds have instructed The People to have." Then he added, "take these animals I have made (ground squirrels, prarie dogs, sparrows) and go to the earth and place them in their proper places."

The youngest of the Sun's children was spoiled in any case and now even more so by the prestige given to him by his special task and became lazy in the things his father had told him to do. Instead of riding a steady rainbow down to earth, the Sun's child slid down a sun ray—a much faster way to go. But in his haste he lost control of the sparrows and they were spread all over the Navajoland. And that is why these birds are everywhere and therefore considered pests.

The Little One, having reached the earth, delighted in the mountains, trees, and animals that inhabited it. He had grown tired of living in the sky and decided to spend some time here, and take time in creating the beast his father had instructed him to make.

He piled up two groupings of soil and like his father, called to the Spirit People to breathe life into them. The wind of life came and from the earth rose two identical creatures designed out of the memory of the Little One. These creatures were lighter, smaller, and more domestic than the rock creatures his father had created. He looked at them with proudness although they were not exactly they way they needed to be: their manes were too long, their hooves too wide and ears large and floppy—much like the donkeys we know of today.

He spent many a long day in play with his new creatures and this made the other pets of the earth to grow jealous and angry—even the otters and other animals that existed in the world before this one joined in the protest. They said: "Little One, why have you forsaken us for these two you have just created? Some of us were made by your father and some of us were here much before the time of these two. They are not so special; we want to challenge them!" They repeated their request three more times and waited for an answer.

So, the Little One thought on this and said: "Yes, you are right. Tomorrow we will have a race around the horizon. The winner will truly be my special one and I will give him a special name."

The group of animals accepted the idea as fair and departed, readying themselves for the race to follow. But The Little One never intended for any of the other animals to beat his chosen creatures—and he also knew that in their present state they would never win.

So, he called them to him and began to take particular pains in grooming them before they ran the race. In this endeavor, he changed their appearance considerably. He pulled out their manes, straightened out their legs and noses, and thinned out their hooves. Then, he began to shorten and straighten out their ears. At this time one of them said: "I do not want my ears like this; leave them as they are." And he did so.

But the Little One was not finished. He was still afraid that one of his prized ones would not win. So, calling on his father, he gathered a group of Rainbow People to place beneath the hooves of the more carefully groomed of his creatures—surely this would make him the victor!

The next day, all the animals gathered for the race. In their jealousy, the earth animals didn't notice the considerable changes in the Little One's creatures. The race began.

During the first few laps of the race, Little One was disappointed and confused because his two animals seemed to meander around and sniff the ground and each other with their new noses. He called out to them: "Why do you two not run with the others?" And they replied: "We are interested in the new things you have given to us." And they continued to procrastinate.

The Sun's youngest became quite worried, for it was now the last lap of the race—the horizon was drawing closer. But just at that moment, his two leaped on their rainbow spectrums and were ahead of the crowd. The short-eared creature won, with his brother quickly behind.

The animals all gathered beneath the House of the Sun, at Mount Taylor, to hear this special name the son of the Sun would give to the victor. The Little One called out: "You all raced well, but this is the creature that won and he will be called 'horse'." The other of his favorites remained in the state he preferred and was later named a jackass, or donkey.

At this time the Bearer of the Sun was watching what was happening below, and was interested in this horse. He dipped the sky down to the earth and allowed his son and the horse to return to his house for him to examine.

"This is a fine creature you have created, my son," he said. "I would like to have many for myself—and for The People as The Little Winds instructed."

At this time, Changing Woman appeared and told them how to populate the earth with horses. She gave them a bag of yellow pollen and whispered the words of reproduction in the Sun's ear.

Following her instructions he created a large herd of horses. And, using rainbows delivered a great many of them to The People. His quest had been fulfilled and The People rejoiced in their new earthly beast.

CHACO CANYON
AND HOW THE
MEXICANS CAME TO BE

N avajo Singers have always told the story of how their Athapascan ancestors, the "original Navajo," first arrived in old Dine Tah (the area of their first settlement or "old" Navajoland; Dinetah, as used in this work, later referred to that larger area they occupied when the Bilagaana arrived in the Southwest and, today, as the land occupied by present-day Navajos). They arrived as poor wanderers and not all in one group. Later, as we shall see, still more of their kind came from the West Coast, after, the myth tales tell us, Changing Woman had gone there to live on an island in the Pacific Ocean.

At any rate, the Navajo Singers, the "keepers of the stories" or historians, have always said that when the first Navajo ancestors arrived in the Dine Tah area in northwestern New Mexico the people of Chaco Canyon were building Pueblo Bonito. This first contact with the Anasazi of Chaco (Tse Tigai, meaning White Rock in Navajo which became Chacra in Spanish and, of course, Chaco, in English) came about AD 950. (Building actually began in Chaco a hundred years earlier). Obviously this early contact with the advanced Anasazi culture made a lasting impact on the poor Athapascan or Dine people, changing the way they lived, the way they worshipped and probably the way they thought. There are easily a dozen tales and fragments of others still existing that tell of events pertaining to those early contact days. This and the two tales that follow are all "Chaco tales."

In its full bloom, c. 900-1200 AD, the Anasazi Culture was the most advanced culture in all North America. They were builders, the Anasazi, and spread out from north central Arizona, into Utah and Colorado, and east of the Rio Grande in New Mexico (I differ with those historians who say the Pueblos are the descendants of the Anasazi and let it go at that; the Anasazi of the Four Corners area and the people who became the ancestors of the Rio Grande Pueblos—Toas, Acoma, for instance—were thriving at the same time and shared enough in common to be considered a part of the same culture—the Anasazi). The Anasazi built their "Cliff Dwellings" high up on the sides of sometimes narrow canyons, on the tops of mesas or, as in the case of Chaco, along the bottoms of shallow canyons. These ranged in size from small, one room affairs, to "apartment buildings" of over twelve hundred rooms and five or six storeys in height.

The Anasazi were farmers and very good at it. They evolved a rich and complex ceremonial life with the more sacred of their ceremonials being celebrated in kivas, usually round and similar to both the pit houses of their early days and the early Navajo hogan.

They so-called mystery of "whatever happened to the Anasazi" and especially the people of Chaco, is one of those self-perpetuating tales that seem to keep a a lot of magazine writers busy. Partially, at least, there is a simple answer: the irrigation farming wore out the land and following two prolonged droughts and subsequent years of heavy rainfall which cut deep into the runoff canyons (and far below the irrigation system connections) the people dispersed.

There also is evidence to support the thesis of serious internal problems. Chaco was the center of a very extented support system; outlier villages lay in every directions and especially to the west, south and north. We now know, as the result of satellite photography, twenty to thirty foot wide roads ran in a direct path to the outlier villages. Altogether these roads served some 60,000 square miles. Interestingly, many of the roads were parallel; the "Great North Road" consisted of not one but two sets of parallel roads which are visible on aerial photographs. The sets are spaced less than fifty feet apart and the two sets are separated by roughly 100 to 130 feet. Archaeologist Fred L. Nials has suggested the possibility that there were different roads for different classes of society. And that suggests a strictly structured class society that would eventually implode, as has been suggested was the fate of Chaco by other researchers.

The longest road discovered so far, in the four hundred mile network, was one that ran nearly a hundred miles into Colorado. These roadways were shored up in low places by masonry, dug below the existing surface in many places and did not veer or curve. Changes of direction were accomplished by a "dog leg" turn and when they came to a mountain they didn't go around it, the road was built in a direct path over it. Now that is the real mystery of Chaco, the building of fourteen pueblos there and the man hours it took to build not only the outliers but the roads to them.

There is no evidence, contrary to what you'll find stated in some of the histories done more than twenty years ago, of warfare made on Chaco and the outliers by "wandering tribes." That usually refers to the Navajo. The very idea that poor, wandering hunters, who traveled in small unorganized groups, could make war on these stone cities is, and always has been, ludicrous.

Chaco seems to have been a seat of government, a religious center and also a storage center for food. It certainly wasn't a burial ground. Pueblo Bonito housed, at its peak, a thousand people and was occupied for over 250 years; yet only a dozen or so burials have been found in the vicinity. Archeologists have suggested that some of the larger buildings, and some of these were of more than a hundred rooms, were used for storing grains and other foods and were not used as living quarters.

There were three centers of Anasazi culture: Mesa Verde in Colorado, Kayenta in Arizona and, Chaco Canyon in New Mexico. The Shoshonean-speaking people of Kayenta have been referred to as the "poor relatives" of the Anasazi; their buildings were not as well constructed, the ceremonial life seems somewhat less developed in comparison to that of other sites, and there is less evidence of the far flung trading activity found at Mesa Verde and particularly at Chaco. The Kayenta people, about 1300, moved south and became the Hopi. The people of Mesa Verde probably did move to the Rio Grande area and they and/or some of the people from Chaco probably built Kwastiyukwa in the Jemez Mountains, and possibly the huge Tyuonyi Pueblo with its 250 ground floor rooms now located in the Bandelier National Monument, New Mexico.

It is logical to assume that some of the people of Chaco—and there was a great many of them as most estimates place the population anywhere from 7,000 to around 13,000 at various times—also moved to the Rio Grande. It is also safe to assume some of them moved south and joined the Zuni because Zuni priests and historians tell us they did.

And it is just to as logical to assume that many inter-married with the Athaspascans and became the people we know today as the Navajo. The Navajo say, in several of their myth tales, that is what happened.

I was recently told that the story that follows had to come into being after Chaco was deserted; even after the Spanish or "Mexicans" arrived in New Mexico. Otherwise how would the Navajo have known the word "Mexican?" The root word for Mexican and Mexico is from the Uto-Aztecan language and referred to a people of Central Mexico. Dozens of artifacts from Central Mexico have been found in the ruins of Chaco and dated prior to the total aban-donment of the series of connecting pueblos in the 1200s. The people of Chaco were trading with the Toltecs and Tula, the city that was the center of that culture in Cen-tral Mexico, long before the Aztecs came into power and a couple of centuries before Cortez stumbled upon Tenochtitlan (Mexico City). The Navajos learned the word from their Chaco ancestors, of course. In any case they had very little early verbal contact with the Spanish of New Mexico who never referred to themselves as "Mexicans" then, nor do they now. More than likely the "Creation of the Mexican" was added to the Nohoilpi tale after the Spanish arrived into New Mexico.

The Navajos retained their Athapascan language but ob-viously adopted the place-fixed religion of their ancestors of Tse Tigai and added to their "myth tales." Where else could their very complex religion—that "works" only within the sacred mountains that surround Dinetah and which also contained the entire Anasazi culture—have come from?

In any case, this is the Navajo's tale of where the Mex-icans came from. But first a quote from Navajo Singer

Manuelito Begay: "There is no mystery about Chaco; our grandfathers married women there and our grandmothers married there also; we are the Anasazi."

THE GAMBLER NOHOILPI, THE GOD OF THE MEXICANS

After First Man and First Woman had made the sacred mountains, the sun and the stars and were pretty much satisfied with the way this Fifth World was looking, they sat out for Spruce Mountain (north central New Mexico), taking Coyote with them for they were all Skin Walkers (Navajo witches) in any case. The people, not knowing what else to do, followed and they also traveled east but at some distance behind First Man, First Woman and Coyote.

At a place called White Spot on the Earth they camped for the night, having given up the idea of keeping up with those others to see where they were going. It was here that a woman gave birth, but her offspring was not like a child at all but was some creature that none of them had seen the likes of before. It was round and had no head. The people had a council and decided to throw it in a gully, which they did. But the monster lived and grew up to be Teelget, who afterwards destroyed so many of The People.

The next day they continued to travel east, and somewhat to the south, following in the tracks of First Man, First Woman and Coyote. When they stopped at a place to camp called Rock Bending Back, another woman gave birth to still another odd looking creature. It had something like feathers growing on both its shoulders and looked like nothing that had ever been seen before. So, the people took it to an alkali bed nearby and cast it away. Still it lived and grew and became the terrible monster Tse'nahale.

Still travelling east and somewhat to the south, they camped the third night near a broad high cliff that was like a wall and here a woman bore yet another strange creature. It had no head, but had a long, pointed end where the head should be. The People placed this monster in a hole in the cliff and sealed it up with stone. They left it there to die but it grew up and became the destroyer Tse'tahotsiltali.

The fourth night they stopped at a place called Rock With Black Hole and twins were born to a woman. The twins were round with one end tapering to a point. There were no signs of limbs or head, but there were depressions which had somewhat the appearance of eyes. The People lay them on the ground and the next day they moved on, abandoning them. The twins grew up, however, and became the Binaye Ahani, who slew with their eyes.

All of these monsters, and still others who were born as the people traveled about there in search of creatures like themselves were the consequence of the transgressions of the women in the Fourth World, which took place when they were separated from the men. Still other monsters were born on the march east and still others sprang from the blood that had been shed during the birth of the first monsters and they all grew up to become enemies and destroyers of The People.

Next The People journeyed until they came to a place called Water In A Narrow Gully, and here they remained for thirteen years, making farms and planting corn, beans and pumpkins every spring.

From that place The People moved to a place called Standing White Rock. They lived there for thirteen more years, and it was during this time that First Woman, First Man and Coyote left them for good and went on to Spruce Mountain, which was not far away, to live. Then they moved to White On Face Of Cliff and here, once more, they remained for thirteen years. It was during this time that the monsters began to devour The People.

From White On The Face Of Cliff they moved to the neighborhood of Kin Tyel (there are over 400 "Bonito phrase" Chaco structures; this one has never been identified) in the Chaco Canyon (New Mexico), where the ruins of the great pueblo still stand. When the Navajos arrived in the Chaco Canyon area, the Kisani (the Anasazi) had already arrived and were in the process of building the great pueblo we call Tse Biyah Anii'ah i (Pueblo Bonito), but had not yet finished it. The reason the Pueblos were building Kin Tyel (sometimes confused with Pueblo Bonito in the myth tales) was to release some of their people from bondage.

A short time before a divine gambler named Nohoilpi (He Who Wins Men) had descended among the Pueblos from the heavens. He was a son of Sun Bearer and had been sent there with divine powers in gambling to win two large turquoises, as large as a man's head, that Sun desired. But upon winning them he had refused to give them up and began abusing his power to win people as slaves in order to building a great building—Kin Tyel—for himself.

Nohoilpi's talisman was also a great piece of turquoise. When he came he challenged the Pueblos to all sorts of games of chance and contests and in all of these he was successful. Not only did he win their property but he also won their women, their children, and finally some of the men themselves. After he had accumulated much of their property and many of the Pueblos as slaves, he told them he would give everything back if they would build a great house for him. So when the Navajos came into that country the Pueblos were busy building Kin Tyel in order that they might release their relatives and their property from He Who Wins Men. They were also busy making a racetrack and preparing for all kinds of games of chance and skill.

But in spite of their losses, the Pueblos continued to gamble with Nohoilpi. People came from other pueblos and gambled away not only their valuables, but also their women, children and finally themselves. The Navajos, observing all this, tried to keep count of Nohoilpi's winnings but people came in such numbers to Chaco that it became impossible. Of course with the labor of all the slaves who had lost themselves to Nohoilpi, it was not long until the great Kin Tyel was finished.

Now the Navajos had been merely spectators of the games and had never taken part. But one day the voice of the beneficial grandfather of the gods, Hasteyalti (Talking God) was heard faintly in the distance crying his usual call—hu'hu'hu'hu', similar to the coo-coo of the dove. His voice was heard as it is always heard, four times, each time nearer and nearer, and immediately after the last call, which was loud and clear, Hasteyalti appeared at the door of the hut of a young childless couple.

Hasteyalti told the young couple that the people of Ki'ndotliz (Blue House Pueblo) had gambled with Nohoilpi and lost two great shells, the greatest treasures of the pueblo. He went on to say that the Tsohanoai, the Sun Bearer, coveted these shells and had asked the gambler, for them as well as the two turquoises as large as a man's head he'd been sent to win but had been refused and now the Sun was angry. Because of this, Hasteyalti said, twelve days after his visit certain gods would meet in the mountains, in a place he designated, to hold a great council.

He then invited the young man to be present at the council and disappeared.

The young Navajo man kept count of the passing days, and on the twelfth day he travelled to the appointed place where he found a great assemblage of the gods. Besides Hasteyalti, there were Hastehogan and his son, Nlch'i (Wind), Chahalgel (Darkness), Beeka'li (Bat) Tl'ish (Snake), Tsilkali (Little Bird), Naazi'si (Gopher) and many others. Not only were the gods tired of this Nohoilpi, but many of the pets belonging to this gambler were also dissatisfied with their lot and longed to be freed. Nlch'i had spoken to them and they had come to enter the plot against their master. All that night the gods danced and sang and performed mystic rites for the purpose of giving the young Navajo man powers as a gambler, equal to those of Nohoilpi. When morning came they washed him with yucca suds, dried him with corn meal, dressed him in clothes exactly like those of the gambler and in every way made him look as much like Nohoilpi as possible. Then the Navajo set out to best the gambler, with the help of the various gods. They arrived at the brow of Chaco Canyon at sunrise the next morning.

Nohoilpi had two wives, who were the prettiest women in the whole land. Wherever they went each of them carried a stick in her hand on which something was tied as a sign that she was the wife of the great gambler.

It was the custom of Nohoilpi's wives to go to a nearby spring each morning at sunrise to fetch water. That morning the young Navajo followed one of the wives to the spring and, as he was dressed and adorned to represent her husband, she let him approach her. When she discovered her error, she deemed it prudent to say nothing and let him follow her into the house. As he entered he observed that many of the slaves had assembled, having heard that trouble was brewing for Nohoilpi. When the gambler saw the stranger, who looked so much like himself, follow his wife into the house, his face became clouded with anger.

"Have you come to gamble with me?" he asked the young intruder. He repeated the question four times and each time the Navajo answered, "No."

In the meantime the party of gods, who had been watching from above, came down among the people and dressed two young boys, nadleeh, who had the gift of impersonating women, in costumes similar to those worn by the wives of the gambler. When these two mock-women entered the gambler's house along with a great many people from the neighboring pueblos, the Navajo pointed at them and said: "I will bet my wives against your wives."

Nohoilpi accepted the wager and they played the game of thirteen chips. (The game is played with thirteen flat pieces of wood, colored red on one side and white on the other. Success depends on the number of chips which, when thrown upwards, fall with the white sides up.) The gambler tossed the chips first and turned up many white chips and a few red ones. When the Navajo tossed the chips into the air, Bat, who had hidden himself in the ceiling, grasped them and tossed down thirteen chips that were white on both sides, and so the Navajo won the wives of Nohoilpi.

Next they went outside and wagered on the game nanzoz (a game where a hoop is rolled along the ground and long poles are thrown after it to make it fall). Great Snake had hidden himself in the hoop and caused it to fall on the Navajo's pole and again the gambler was defeated.

Very angry now, the gambler pointed to two small trees and challenged the Navajo to the game of tsinbetsil (or push-on-the-wood, a contest in which the opponents find trees of equal size and push against them, the first to cause the tree to be torn from its roots and fall being the winner). But the Navajo insisted that larger trees be found and they finally agreed on two of good size that grew closely together. Wind told the Navajo which tree to select. The gambler strained with all his might at his tree but he could not move it. When the Navajo's turn came he shoved his tree prostrate with little effort for its roots had been severed by Gopher.

Then followed a variety of games, on one of which Nohoilpi staked his wealth in shells and precious stones, his houses and his slaves—and lost all. The victor ordered all the shells, beads and precious stones and the great shells and the large turquoises desired by Sun brought forth. He gave the the beads to Hasteyalti for distribution among the gods, and the two great shells and the two large turquoises were given to Tsohanoai, the Sun Bearer, who desired them for his house.

After losing all he had, Nohoilpi was very angry and bemoaned his fate and cursed his enemies. "I will kill you all with lightning. I will send war and disease among you. May cold freeze you! May the fire burn you! May the waters drown you!" he cried.

Wind decided that Nohoilpi had cursed enough and told the Navajo to put an end to his angry words. So the young Navajo called the gambler to him and said: "You have bet yourself and lost; you are now my slave and must do my bidding. You are not a god, for my power has prevailed against yours."

The young Navajo had been given a magic bow by Hasteyalti, the Bow of Darkness, which he bent upwards, and placing the string on the ground bade the gambler stand on the string; then he shot Nohoilpi up into the sky.

Up and up Nohoilpi flew like an arrow, growing smaller

and smaller until he disappeared altogether. He flew up in the sky until he came to the home of Klehanoai, the God Who Carries The Moon and is thought by the Navajos to be identical with the Christian God of the Americans and Mexicans, a very old man who dwells in a long row of stone houses. When Nohoilpi arrived at the house of Klehanoai he told him what had happened in the lower world, saying, "Now I am poor and this is why I have come to see you."

"You need be poor no longer," said Klehanoai, "for I will provide for you."

Then the Moon God made all sorts of new kinds of animals for Nohoilpi: sheep, asses, horses, swine, goats and fowls. He also gave him bayeta (Spanish for baize which the Navajos obtained from the Spaniards) and other cloths of bright colors, more beautiful than those woven by his slaves at Kintyel. Then he made a new people for the gambler to rule over, the Mexicans, and sent him back to this world again. But he descended far to the south of his former home and reached the earth in Mexico, where the moon god had placed the new people.

Nohoilpi's people increased greatly in Mexico and after a while they began to move toward the North and build towns along the Rio Grande and soon enslaved the Pueblos who lived there. That is how the Mexicans and their domestic animals came about and why they were, from the beginning, the enemies of the Navajo.

A WORLD OF EAGLES

This is another story which takes place, at least in part, at Chaco, but becomes, in the telling, a story of the Sixth World. It is the only story I know of that takes us beyond this, the Fifth World. It is a part of a ceremony called Bead Way, that, as far as I know, has been lost. However, I was recently told, while this work was in progress, of a Singer who lives over in the New Mexico "Checkerboard" area who performs a shortened version of the Bead Way. I have known one Singer who had a grandfather who "owned" the Bead Way ceremony and while he heard it a few times as a child and knew the story of the eagles, he had not mastered the Bead Way or any of the myth tales that accompany it. I read the Eagle Story that follows to him, which, of course, is adapted from the one collected by Washington Matthews over a hundred years ago. He suggested several minor but important corrections that were incorporated in this version of the story.

The first time I went to Chaco the present "improved" road didn't exist. It may not seem to be all that improved to the people who use it but compared to the dusty, potholed, rock filled truck trail that we had to use before, it is a highway. Upon first seeing Pueblo Bonito, which is actually an outlier, I was speechless. I had seen the Toltec-Aztec and several of the Mayan ruins in central America but I *expected* to be impressed by them. Here, in the middle of a high desert in New Mexico, were the remains of a building that made my eyes doubt what they were seeing. I do remember the question of "who" and "how" kept popping into my head. The "who" has pretty much been answered in my mind; I'm not sure the "how" ever will be. To me the "how" of the building of Chaco—and Mesa Verde, too, for that matter—is a far greater mystery than the building of the pyramids of Egypt and Central America. They had lots of people and manpower there; the highest population estimate of Chaco runs about 13,000, tops. Not many people to build about fourteen towns and apartment buildings of stone stacked atop stone for up to five storeys. And most of the major building was done within a span of about one hundred years.

A couple of years ago a some friends of mine, Dr. Joanne Daley and her husband, filmmaker David Oyster, moved to Dziltha-Na-O-Ditha-Hle Heath Center, about thirty miles north of Chaco where Joanne is a physician to Navajos. Joanne, the daughter of my good friend and sometimes co-worker, Marianne Ruuth, probably heard me talking about the Navajo when she was still in grade school—which was only about fifteen years ago. While attending medical school at the University of Southern California Joanne served her clinic requirement on the Navajo reservation and decided to go back there and practice upon getting her MD.

While visiting her mother in Los Angeles at Christmas, 1989, I questioned Joanne about her first impression of Chaco. Her answer:

"I didn't believe my eyes at first. It was pure magic. Actually, I saw it long before I went there to live; it was while David was working on "Cosmos" (the PBS television series). I was just overwhelmed and then a most interesting and strange thing happened. We went into one of the old buildings that really hasn't been explored that much. It was high up. A strong wind came up very suddenly, as if from nowhere. The wind was followed by a sound, a high, whine that hurt the ears. It sounded like voices but it was unlike anything I'd ever heard before. Or since. It was as if I was being told I was at a place I shouldn't be."

Well, I knew exactly the sound Joanne was talking about and so do many others who have visited Anasazi ruins. It first happened to me in 1969 at Mummy House. I went up into Mummy House with Marianne Greenwood and Larry Issacs, Jr. We hadn't been there more than ten minutes and I really don't remember a wind. But that high pitched, whining sound came suddenly and with great force. And it sounded like a thousand screaming voices, eerie and as if in great pain. Mummy House is a large ruin about three hundred feet up in a Canyon del Muerto wall. It took us about twenty minutes to climb up there; it took me about five to tumble back down. A few minutes later Marianne Greenwood came tumbling right behind me. "Did you hear it, too?" she asked.

I've never asked Larry if he heard it, that day or any other. But I could tell by the way he looked at us that he knew. Now this is not the sort of thing you usually tell strangers but I've heard that same sound two other times while inside Anasazi ruins. Once I was in a party that included two Navajo women. I could tell by the expression on their faces that they heard it, too.

I've questioned several people about the "sound" but other than Marianne and Joanne I've only had one white person, a wonderful woman who teaches anthropology at a West Coast University and who once wrote a wonderful book about the Navajo, admit hearing it. Her reply: "On, that high pitched sound. Of course I've heard it. Anyone who has been there and hasn't heard it had their ears shut." Unfortunately this is the last "introduction" I'm (re)writing to this book, it is Christmas day, 1989, this book is going to press next week and I can't reach that dear lady to get permission to use her name. Most people who know about anthropology, Navajos and such will figure it out quickly enough and the name wouldn't really matter to much of anyone else.

THE WORLD
OF THE EAGLES

This happened in the days when the Kisani (Anasazi or Pueblos) were still dwelling at Chaco. The Navajos, then, were very poor and lived scattered about the countryside in small camps. This was after the Dineh and the Kisani, who were much more wealthy in all goods, had been in the Fifth World for many years.

One day two young men, one from the pueblo of Kin Tyel (Broad House) and one from the pueblo of Kin Dotliz, left Chaco Canyon to hunt deer, traveling north. All day they went about, there toward Spruce Mountain. They camped that night, having found no game, and the next day started back toward home. Weary and disheartened, they traveled slowly. The sun had moved toward the western sea, where Changing Woman now dwelt on her island of Turquoise, when the two young men of Chaco saw a war eagle soaring overhead. They stopped to watch his flight.

The eagle moved slowly, in a direct manner, toward the south. Now, in those days eagles were very rare and it is possible the young men had never before seen such a being. At any rate they were highly impressed and continued to watch the bird until it was but a speck in the sky. They had not gone much farther when they again saw the eagle, now flying overhead from east to west. Sometime later, they again saw the eagle with the body of some small animal carried in its talons. This time the bird again came from the north, flying south again in the direction they were traveling. And again it moved slowly away, growing smaller and smaller, dwindling again to a speck. Still they watched in the last light of day and saw the bird descend to the top of a place called Tse'deza (Standing Rock, possibly the same site where The People were camping when First Man, First Woman and Coyote left them in the last story, and just before they came upon Chaco). They suspected the eagle had a nest there and marked the spot where they'd last seen it by cutting a forked stick which they stuck into the ground. By crouching in a certain position and sighting, their eyes were directed to the spot. They left then and went home to Chaco Canyon.

As it has been stated eagles were very scarce in the land and it was a wonder to see one. When the young men got home and told the story of their adventure, it became the subject of much conversation and counsel, and at length the people decided to send four men, in the morning, to take sight over the forked stick in order to find out where the eagle lived.

Next morning the four men chosen traveled to the forked stick and sighted over it, and came to the conclusion that the eagle lived on the point of Standing Rock. They went at once to the rock, climbed to the top, and saw the eagle and its young in a cleft on the face of the precipice below them. They remained on top of the rock all day and watched the nest.

When Sun moved down to the earth in the west for his nightly visit with Turquoise Woman they returned home and told the people what they had seen. They had observed two young eagles of different ages in the nest. Of the four men who went on the search, two were from Kin Dotliz and two were from Kin Tyel; therefore people from the two pueblos met in counsel in the kiva, and there it was decided that Kin Dotliz should have the elder of the eagles and Kin Tyel should have the younger.

The only way to reach the nest was to lower a man to it with a rope; yet directly above the nest was an overhanging ledge which the man, descending, would be obliged to pass. It was a dangerous undertaking, and no one could be found to volunteer for it. There lived near Chaco at that time, but outside of the pueblos proper, a family of poor Navajos who subsisted on such food as they could pick up or beg from the Anasazi. Belonging to this family was a young man who was allowed to sweep the rooms of the pueblo and clean ashes from the fireplaces. By this method he lived on grain and leavings from the meals of the Kisani, who had plenty in those days. He was called Nahoditahe, or He Who Picks Up (Like A Bird). The men of Chaco decided they would induce this one to make the dangerous descent on rope to the eagle's nest.

They sent messengers to fetch the poor Navajo. When he arrived they treated him most kindly, asked that he be seated in a place of honor and fed him their best food; they boiled flesh of deer, corn and freshly cooked squash and begged him to keep eating even after he'd had his fill. He finally told his hosts that he was satisfied; that he could eat no more.

"You shall eat of such abundance all your life, and never more have to scrape for grains of corn among the dirt, if you will do as we desire." Then they told him of their plan for capturing the young eagles, and asked him if he were willing to be put in a basket and lowered to the nest with a rope. He was silent. They asked him again and again until they had asked him four times while he sat pondering the problem. At last he answered: "I lead but a poor life at best. Existence is not sweet to a man who always hungers. It would be pleasant to eat such food for the rest of my days, and some time or other I must die in any case. I shall do as you wish."

The following morning they fed him another meal of their best food. They then made a great, strong carrying basket with four corners at the top; they tied a strong rope to each corner, and, collecting a large party, they set out for Standing Rock.

When the party arrived at the top of Tse'deza they tied a long, stout rope to the four attached to the basket. They instructed the Navajo to take the eaglets out of the nest and drop them to the bottom of the cliff. The Dineh then entered the basket and was lowered over the edge of the precipice. They let the rope out slowly till they thought they had lowered him far enough then they stopped; but as he had not yet reached the nest he called out to them to lower him farther. They did so, and as soon as he was on a level with the nest he called to Kisani above to stop.

He was just about to grasp the eaglets and throw them down when Wind whispered to him: "These people of the Pubelos are not your friends. They desire not to feed you with their good food as they promised. If you throw these young eagles down, as they bid you, they will never pull you up again. Get into the eagles' nest and stay there."

When he heard this, he called to those above: "Swing

129

the basket so that it may come nearer the cliff. I cannot reach the nest unless you do so."

So they caused the basket to swing back and forth. When it touched the cliff he held fast to the rock and scrambled into the nest, leaving the empty basket swinging in the air.

The Pueblos saw the empty basket swinging and waited, expecting to see the Navajo get back into it again. But when they had waited a good while and found he did not return they began to speak to him as if he were a dear relation. "My son," said the old men, "Throw down those little eagles." "My elder brother! My younger brother!" the young men shouted, "Throw down those little eagles." They kept up their clamor until nearly sunset; but they never moved the will of the Navajo who was following the instructions of the Holy Wind. He sat in the cleft and never answered them, and when the sun set they ceased calling and went home.

The Navajo saw that in the cleft of the cave, around the nest, four dead animals lay: to the east there was a fawn; to the south a hare; to the west the young of a Rocky Mountain sheep, and to the north a prairie dog. From time to time, when the eaglets felt hungry, they would leave the nest and eat the meat; but the Navajo did not touch it.

Early the next day the Kisani returned and gathered in a great crowd at the foot of the cliff. They remained there all day repeating their entreaties and promises, calling the Navajo by endearing terms, and displaying all kinds of tempting food to his gaze. The young Dineh paid no attention and spoke not a word to them.

They came early again on the third day but this time they came in anger. They no longer called him by friendly names; they no longer made fair promises to him. Instead, they shot fire arrows at the aerie in hopes they would burn the Navajo out; set fire to the nest and compel him to throw it and the eaglets down to those waiting below. But he remained watchful and active, and whenever a fire arrow entered the cave he quickly seized it and threw it out. The Kisani grew even more furious and called him bad names until sunset, when again they went home.

They came again on the fourth day prepared as if going into battle. But this time they had brought more of their kind and shot so many fire arrows at the nest the Navajo could not catch them fast enough. He spoke to the birds, saying: "Can you not help me?"

They rose in the nest, shook their wings, and thew out many little feathers, which fell on the people below. The Navajo thought the birds must be scattering disease on his enemies. When the latter left at sunset they said: "Now we shall leave you where you are, to die of hunger and thirst."

He was there altogether three nights and nearly four days in the cave. For two days the Pueblos had coaxed and flattered him; for two days they had cursed and reviled him, and at the end of the fourth day they went home and left him in the cave to die.

When his tormentors were gone he sat in the cave hungry and thirsty, not knowing what to do, til nightfall. Soon after dark he heard a great rushing sound which approached from one side of the entrance to the cave, made a loud roaring sound for a moment in front, then grew faint in the distance at the other side. Thus four times the sound came and went, growing louder each time it passed, and at length the male Eagle lit on the aerie. Soon the sounds were repeated and the female bird, the mother of the eaglets alighted . Turning at once toward the Navajo, she said: "Greetings, my child! Thanks my child! You have not thrown down your younger brothers, Doniki."

The male eagle repeated the same words. They addressed the Navajo by the name of Doniki but afterwards they named him Kinniki, after the chief of all the Eagles in the sky. He had now been four days without food or water and could only reply: "I am hungry. I am thirsty."

The male eagle opened his sash and took out a small white cotton cloth which contained a little corn meal, and he took out a small owl of white shell no bigger than the palm of the hand. When the Navajo saw this he said: "Give me the water first, for I am famishing with thirst."

"No," replied the eagle. "Eat first and then you shall have something to drink."

The Eagle then drew forth from among his tail feathers a small plant called eltindzakas (horse tail), which has many joints and grows near streams. The joints were all filled with water. The Eagle mixed a little of the water with some of the meal in the shell and handed the mixture to the Navajo. The latter ate and ate, until he was satisfied, but he could not diminish in the least the contents of the shell vessel. When he was done eating there was as much in the shell cup as there was when he began. He handed it back to the Eagle, the latter emptied it with one sweep of his finger, and it remained empty. Then the Eagle put the eltindzakas plant to the Navajo's lips as if it were a wicker bottle, and the Navajo drank his fill.

On the previous nights, while lying in the cave, the Navajo had slept between the eaglets in the nest to keep himself warm and shelter himself from the wind, and this plan had been of some help to him; but on this night the great Eagles slept one on each side of him, and he felt as warm as if he had slept among robes of fur. Before the Eagles lay down to sleep each took off his plumes, which formed a single garment, opening in front, and revealed a form like that of a human being.

The Navajo slept well that night and did not awaken

till he heard a voice calling at the top of the cliff: "Where are you? The day has dawned. It is growing late. Why have not you greeted the dawn?"

At the sound of this voice the Eagles awoke also and put on their robes of plumage. Presently a great number of birds were seen flying before the opening of the cave and others were heard calling to one another overhead. There were many kinds of Eagles and Hawks. Some of the large birds of prey were there. Those on top of the rock sang:

> "Kinnakiye, there he sits.
> When they fly up,
> We shall see him.
> He will flap his wings."

One of the Eagles brought a dress of the plumes of his kind and was about to put it on the Navajo when the others questioned his actions, and they had a long argument as to whether they should dress him in the garment of the Eagles or not; but at length they all flew away without giving him the dress. When they returned they had thought of another plan for taking him out of the cave. Laying him on his face, they put a streak of crooked lightning under his feet, a sunbeam under his knees, a piece of straight lightning under his chest, another under his hands, and a rainbow under his forehead.

An Eagle then seized each end of these six supports— twelve eagles in all—and they flew with the Navajo and the eaglets away from the aerie. They circled around twice with their burden before they reached the level of the top of the cliff. They circled round twice more ascending, and then flew toward the south, still going upwards. When they got above the top of Tsoodzil (Mt. Taylor), they circled four times more, until they almost touched the sky. Then they began to tire and breathe hard, and cried out: "We are weary. We can fly no farther."

The voice of one, unseen to the Navajo, cried from above: "Let go of your burden."

The Eagles released their hold on the supports, and the Navajo felt himself descending swiftly toward the earth. But he had not fallen far when he felt himself seized around the waist and chest, and felt something twining itself around his body. A moment later he beheld the heads of two arrow snakes (the coach whip) looking at him over his shoulders. The arrow snakes bore him swiftly upwards, up through the sky hole and landed him safely on the surface of the Upper (The Sixth) World above the sky.

When he looked around, he observed four dwellings. A white pueblo in the east; a blue pueblo in the south, a yellow pueblo in the west, and a black pueblo in the north. Wolf was the chief of the eastern pueblo, Blue Fox of the southern, Puma of the western and Big Snake of the northern. The Navajo was left at liberty to go where he chose, but Wind whispered into his ear and said: "Visit, if you wish, all the pueblos except that of the north. Chicken Hawk and other bad characters dwell there."

Next he observed that a war party was readying itself, and soon after his arrival the warriors went forth. What enemies they sought he could not learn. He entered several of the houses, was well treated wherever he went, and given abundance of bread and other good food to eat. He saw that in their homes the Eagles were just like ordinary people down in the lower world. As soon as they entered their pueblos they took off their feather suits, hung them up on pegs and poles, and went around in white cotton clothing which they wore underneath their feathers when in flight. He visited all the pueblos except the black one in the north. In the evening the warriors returned. They were received with tears and loud wailing, for many who were received with tears and loud wailing, for many who had gone out to face the enemy had not returned. They had been slain in battle.

In a few days another war party was organized, and this time the Navajo was determined to accompany it. When the warriors started on the trail he followed them. "Where are you going?" they asked.

"I wish to be one of your party," he replied.

They laughed at him and said: "You are a fool to think you can go to war against such dreadful enemies as those we fight. We can move as fast as the wind, yet our enemies can move faster. If they are able to overcome us, what chance have you, a mere man, for your life?"

Hearing this, he remained behind, but the war party had not traveled far when he hurried after them. When he overtook them, which he soon did, they spoke to him angrily, told him more firmly than before how helpless he was, and how great his danger, and ordered him to return to the villages. Again he halted; but as soon as they were out of sight he began to run after them, and he came up with them at the place where they had encamped for the night. Here they gave him of their food, and again they scolded him, and sought to dissuade him from accompanying them.

In the morning, when the warriors resumed their march, he remained behind on the camping ground, as if he intended to return; but as soon as they were out of sight he proceeded again to follow them. He had not traveled far when he saw smoke coming up out of the ground, and approaching the smoke he found a smokehole, out of which stuck an old ladder, yellow with smoke, such as we seen in the Pueblo dwellings today. He looked down through the hole and beheld, in a subterranean chamber beneath, a strange looking old woman with a big mouth. Her teeth were not set in her head evenly and regularly, like those of an Indian; they protruded from her mouth, were set at a distance from one another, and were curved like the claws of a bear. She was Nastse Estsan, the Spider Woman. She invited him into her house, and he passed down the ladder.

When he got inside, the Spider Woman showed him four large wooden hoops—one in the east colored white, one in the south colored blue, one in the west colored yellow and one in the north colored black.

Attached to each hoop were a number of decayed, ragged feathers. "These feathers," said she, "were once beautiful plumes, but now they are old and dirty. I want some new plumes to adorn my hoops and you can get them for me. Many of the Eagles will be killed in the battle to which you are going, and when they die you can pluck out the plumes and bring them to me. Have no fear of the enemies. Would you know who they are the Eagles fight? They are only the bumblebees and the tumbleweeds."

She gave him a long black cane and said: "With this you can gather the tumbleweeds into a pile and then you can set them on fire. Spit the juice of tsildailgisi (wild tobacco) at the bees and they cannot sting you. But before you burn the tumbleweeds gather some of the seeds, and when you have killed the bees take some of their nests. You will need these things when you return to the earth."

When Spider Woman had done speaking the Navajo left to do as she had instructed.

He traveled on, and soon caught up with the warriors where they were hiding behind a little hill and preparing for battle. Some were putting on their plumes; others were painting and adorning themselves. From time to time one of their number would creep cautiously to the top of the hill and peep over; then he'd run back and whisper: "There are enemies. They await us."

The Navajo went to the top of the hill and peered over; but he could see no enemy. He saw only a dry, sandy flat, covered in one place with sunflowers, and in another place with dead weeds; for it was now late autumn in the world above.

Soon the Eagles were all ready for the fight. They raised their war cry and charged over the hill into the sandy plain. The Navajo remained behind the hill, peeping over to see what would occur. As the warriors approached the plain a whirlwind arose; a great number of tumbleweeds ascended with the wind and surged around madly through the air; and, at the same time, from among the sunflowers a cloud of bumblebees arose. The Eagles charged through the ranks of their enemies, and when they had passed to the other side they turned around and charged back again. Some spread their wings and soared aloft to attack the tumbleweeds that had gone with the whirlwind. From time to time the Navajo noticed the dark body of an Eagle falling down through the air. When the combat had continued for some time, the Navajo noticed a few of the Eagles running toward the hill where he lay watching. In a moment some more came running toward him, and soon after the whole party of Eagles, all that was left of it, rushed past him, in a disorderly retreat, in the direction whence they had come, leaving many slain on the field. Then the wind fell; the tumbleweeds lay quiet again on the sand, and the bumblebees disappeared among the sunflowers.

When all was quiet, the Navajo walked down to the sandy flat, and, having gathered some of the seeds and tied them up in a corner of his shirt, he collected the tumbleweeds into a pile, using his black wand. Then he took out his fire drill, started a flame and burnt up the whole pile. He gathered some tsildilgisi, as Spider Woman had told him, chewed it, and went in among the sunflowers. Here the bees gathered around him in a great swam, and sought to sting him; but he spat the juice of the tsildigisi at them and stunned with it all that he struck. Soon the most of them lay helpless on the ground, and the others fled in fear. He went around with his black wand and killed all that he could find. He dug into the ground and got out some of their nests and honey; he took a couple of the young bees and tied their feet together, and all these things he put into the corner of his blanket. When the bees were conquered he did not forget the wishes of his friend, Spider Woman; he went around among the dead eagles and plucked as many plumes as he could grasp in both hands.

He set out on his return journey and soon got back to the house of Spider Woman. He gave her the plumes and she said: "Thank you, my grandchild, you have brought me the plumes that I have wanted to adron my walls, and you have done a great service to your friends, the Eagles, because you have slain their enemies."

When she had spoken he again set out on his journey and slept that night on the trail. Late the next morning he arrived back at the towns of the Eagles. As he approached he heard from afar the cries of the mourners, and when he entered the place the people gathered around him and said: "We have lost many of our kinsmen, and we are wailing for them; but we have been also mourning for you, for those who returned told us you had been killed in a fight."

He made no reply, but took from his blanket the two young bumblebees and swung them around his head. All the people were terrified and ran, and they did not stop running until they got inside their houses. In a little while they got over their fear, came slowly out of the houses and crowded around the Navajo again. A second time he swung the bees around his head, and a second time the people ran away in terror; but this time they only went as far as the front walls of their houses, and soon they returned again to the Navajo. The third time that he swung the bees around his head they were still less frightened, ran but halfway to their houses and returned very soon. The fourth time that he swung the bees they only retreated a few steps. When their courage came back to them, he placed the bees on the ground; took out the seeds of the tumbleweeds and laid them on the ground beside the bees, and then he said to the Eagle People: "My friends, here are the children of your enemies."

There was great rejoicing among the people when they heard this, and this one said: "It is well. They have slain my brother," and another one said: "It is well. They have slain my father." And still another said: "It is well. They have slain my sons." Then Great Wolf, chief of the white pueblo said: "I have two beautiful maiden daughters whom I shall give to you." Then Fox, chief of the blue pueblo in the south, promised him two more maidens, and the chiefs of the other pueblos promised him two each, so that eight beautiful maidens were promised to him in marriage.

The chief of the white pueblo now conducted the Navajo to his house and into spacious and beautiful quarters, the finest the poor man had ever seen. The apartment had smooth walls, nicely coated with white earth, a large fireplace, mealing stones, beautiful pots and water jars, and all the conveniences and furnishings of a beautiful Pueblo home. The leader of the white pueblo said to him: "My son-in-law, this house is yours."

The principal men of all the pueblos came to visit him

and thanked him for the great service he had done for them. Then his maidens from the yellow house came in bringing him corn meal; the maidens from the black house entered bring soapweed, and the maidens from the white house, where he was staying, came baring a large bowl of white shell. A suds of the soapweed was prepared in the shell bowl. The maidens of the white house washed his head with the suds; the maidens of the black house washed his limbs and feet, and those of the yellow house dried him with corn meal. When the bath was finished the maidens went out; but they returned at dark, accompanied this time by maidens of the blue house. Each of the eight maidens carried a large bowl of food, and each bowl contained food of a different kind. They placed the eight bowls before the Navajo, and he ate of all until he was satisfied. Then they brought in beautiful robes and blankets and spread them on the floor floor for his bed.

Next morning the Navajo went over to the sky hole, taking with him the young bees and the seeds of the tumbleweeds. To the former he said: "God down to the land of the Navajos and multiply there. My people will make use of you in the days to come; but if you ever cause them sorrow and trouble, as you have caused the people of this world, I shall again destroy you." As he spoke he flung them down to the earth. Then taking the seeds of the tumbleweeds in his hands, he spoke to them as he had spoken to the bees and threw them down through the sky hole. The honey of the bees and the seeds of the tumbleweeds are now used in the rites of yoi hatal, or the Bead Chant.

The Navajo remained in the pueblos of the Eagle People twenty-four days, during which time he was taught the songs, prayers, ceremonies and sacrifices of the Eagles, the same as those now known to us in the rite of yoi hatal, the Bead Way, and when he had learned all the people told him it was time for him to return to the earth.

They dressed him in a robe of eagle plumage, such as they wore themselves, and led him to the sky hole. The leader of White House said to him: "When you came up from the lower world you were heavy and had to be carried by others. Henceforth you will be light and can move through the air with your own power." He spread his wings to show that he was ready; the Eagles blew a powerful breath behind him; he went down through the sky hole and was wafted down on his outstretched wings until he landed on the summit of Tsoodzil.

He went back to his relatives among the Navajos but when he entered their hogan everything smelt badly. The odor was intolerable to him and he had to leave and sit outside. His relatives built a medicine lodge for him where he might sit by himself. They bathed his younger brother, dressed him in new clothing and sent him to the new lodge to learn what his elder brother could teach him about the Eagles. The brothers spent twelve days in the lodge together, during which the elder told his story and instructed the younger in all the rites and songs learned.

After this Nahoditahe went to visit the pueblo of Kin Tyel in Chaco Canyon where those Kisini lived that had plotted such treachery toward him; but they did not recognize him now. He was sleek and well fed, and beautifully dressed in the robes given him by the Eagles who had also molded, in beauty, his face and form. It never occurred to the Kisini that this could be the poor beggar they had left to die in the eagles' nest.

He observed that there were now many ill and lame living at Kin Tyel; caused by a disease they had caught form the feathers scattered by the eaglets when they were attacking the nest. "I have a brother," said the Navajo, "who is a potent shaman. He knows a rite that will cure this disease." The people of the pueblo consulted together and concluded to employ his brother to perform the ceremony over their suffering ones.

The Navajo told them he must be one of the first dancers, and that in order to perform the rite properly he must be dressed in a very particular way. He must, he said, be given strings of fine beads—shell and turquoise—sufficient to cover his legs and forearms completely, enough to go around his neck, so that he could not bend his head back, and great strings to pass over the shoulder and under the arm on each side. He must have the largest shell basin to be found in either pueblo to hang on his back, and the one next in size to hang on his chest. He must have the longest and best strings of turquoise to hang on his ears. The Wind told him that the greatest shell basin they had was so large that if he tried to embrace it around the edge, his fingertips would scarcely meet on the opposite side, and that this shell he must insist on having. The next largest shell, Wind told him, was but a little smaller.

Three days after this conference, people began to come in from different pueblos in the Chaco Canyon and from the pueblos on the banks of San Juan—all of these pueblos are now in ruins—and soon a great multitude had assembled. Meantime, too, they collected shells and beads from various pueblos in order to dress the atsalei (first dancer) as he desired. They brought him some great shell basins and told him these were what he wanted for the dance; but he measured them with his arms as Wind had instructed him, and, finding that his hands joined easily when he embraced the shells, he discarded them. They brought him larger and larger shells, and tried to persuade him that such was their largest; but he tried and rejected all. On the last day, with reluctance, they brought him the great shell of Kin Tyel and the great shell of Kin Dotliz. He clasped the first in his arms; his fingers did not meet on the opposite side. He clased the second in his arms, and the tips of his fingers just met.

"These," he said, "are the shells I must wear when I dance."

Four days before the ceremony was to begin, the Kisini sent out messengers to the neighboring camps of Navajos to invite them to witness the exhibition of the last night and to participate in it with some of their own dances. Messengers started for the Navajo camp at the foot of Tsoodzil on the south (near where Cobero is now). On his way he met a messenger, come from Tsoodzil to invite the people of Chaco Canyon to a great Navajo ceremony. (The story of this meeting is told in the Mountain Way ceremony). The messengers exchanged bows and quivers as a sign they had met one another, and the messenger from Kin Tyel returned to his people without being able to get the Navajos from Mt. Taylor to attend. That is reason that on the last night of the great ceremony of yoi hatal (Bead Way), there are but few dances.

On the evening of the last day they built a great circle of branches, such as the Navajos build now for the rites of the Mountain Chant, and a great number of people crowded into the enclosure. They lit fires and dressed the atsalei in all their fine beads and shells just as he desired to be dressed. They then put the great shell of Kin Tyel on his back, and the great shell of Kin Dotliz on his chest, and another fine shell on his forehead. Then the Navajo began to dance, and his brother, the shaman, began to sing, and this was the song he sang:

> The white corn plant's great ear sticks up
> Stay down and eat.
> The blue corn plant's great ear sticks up

Stay down and eat.
The yellow corn plant's great ear sticks up
Stay down and eat.
The black corn plant's great ear sticks up
Stay down and eat.
All colored corn plant's great ear sticks up
Stay down and eat.
The round-eared corn's great ear sticks up
Stay down and eat.

Now this seemed a strange song to the Kisini and they all wondered what it meant but they soon found out. They observed that the dancing Navajo was slowly rising from the ground. First his head and then his shoulders appeared above the heads of the crowd; next his chest and waist; but it was not until his whole body had risen above the level of their heads that they began to realize the loss that threatened them. He was rising toward the sky with the great shell of Kin Tyel and all the wealth of many pueblos in shell beads and turquoise on his body. Then they screamed wildly to him and called him by all sorts of dear names—father, brother, son—to come down again, but the more they called the higher he rose. When his feet had risen above them they observed that a streak of white lightening passed under his feet like a rope, and hung from a dark cloud that gathered above. It was the gods that were lifting him; for thus, the legends say, the gods lift mortals to the sky. When the Kisini found that no persuasions could induce the Navajo to return, some called for ropes that they might seize him and pull him down; but he was soon beyond the reach of their longest rope. Then a shout was raised for arrows that they might shoot him; but before the arrows could come he was lost to sight in the black cloud and was never more seen on earth.

CHANGING WOMAN
AND
WHITE SHELL WOMAN

C hanging Woman is mentioned in many of the myth tales that deal with The People's early years in this, the Fifth World. And I know three slightly varying versions of the tale of her birth, one of which has her and White Shell Woman being created by the gods on Spruce Mountain, still another that places the creation site near the Hopi First Mesa and the one that follows, that has the creation site at Ch'ooli (Gobernador Knob in old Dine Tah; one of the "middle" sacred mountains). The Changing Woman Story is one of the most sacred of Navajo myth tales and is central to the Blessing Way, that ceremony upon which many students of Navajo religion say is the "stalk" of Navajo religion.

In this story First Man and First Woman are still living at White Standing Rock where, in the Gambler story, they had moved on to Spruce Mountain to live. That, of course, was while the monsters or Naye'i were first being born. Here they've been around long enough to devour almost all the people and all of the children.

It really isn't important but this is an example of how

the myth tales may vary slightly from one Singer (or source) to another.

At any rate, it is a wonderful story and certainly one of my favorites and it is, of course, followed by the story of the "twins" born to Changing Woman and her sister, White Shell Woman, who are named Monster Slayer and Born of Water. The story of the Hero Twins is told in several Ways and is represented in more dry paintings than (probably) any of the other gods.

They, too, are the children of the Sun Bearer—that fellow really got around when it came to fathering children— and, as such, were "born" gods and not created. As you shall see, they became very important gods.

Obviously, Changing Woman and White Shell Woman were created to become the mother of the Hero Twins and they, in turn, were charged by the gods with destroy- ing all the monsters that were born as a result of the misbehavior of the women when they were separated from the men in the Fourth World. The alien gods were eating The People, until there were hardly any left and no children exist any longer until birth was given to the Hero Twins.

The Hero Twins, then, made the Fifth World safe by destroying all the monsters. That not only allowed The People to become fruitful but it shaped the world so they could come together as a "new" people or tribe. The word "tribe" is actually a misnomer. The Navajos never did function as a "tribe" and until the Bureau of Indian Af- fairs created the Navajo Tribal Council back in the 1920s, never recognized a "chief" or any other sort of central authority. Clan leaders and local "headmen" earned the respect of their followers through exercising good judge- ment and common sense and were listened to and follow- ed as long as they did so—or until someone a bit wiser came along. As a people the Navajo had language and religion and other traits in common but they found it difficult to understand and ever harder to accept the idea of an overall "chief," king or, for that matter, president, including that mysterious being "Father Washingdon" (sic) .who took over their destiny in the late 1860s.

Now, let us get on with the story telling.

THE SACRED SISTERS

After leaving Chaco Canyon the Navajos had scattered because the monsters (Naye'i) or alien gods had been actively pursuing and devouring The People. Even First Man and First Woman were wandering about not knowing what to do about the fate of The People. Of the group still living at White Standing Rock, there were now only four Navajos left along with First Man, First Woman, Salt Woman and other gods of little importance.

One day, First Woman and Salt Woman were standing below Fluted Rock (New Mexico) and saw Earth and Sky meet. Now, they knew this was a message of the Spirit People but they had not seen this sort of thing since coming to the Fifth World.

They were confused and decided to go to the top of the mountain to see if there was indeed any sign. As they approached the summit, they heard the sound of a crying child.

"What is this I hear, my sister?" First Woman said to Salt Woman.

"It cannot be a child for there are none of The People living up here," Salt Woman returned.

But this sound continued and eventually at the very top of the mountain they found two stone images of people:

one of turquoise and one of white shell.

They wondered what these images meant so they brought them down the hill to show First Man. First Man, studying the images, agreed that this was a message from the Spirit People but he did not know what it meant. Suddenly, though, Hasteyalti, the Talking God, came to them.

In his usual manner his appearance was announced by three calls, each increasing in volume until the fourth call when he materialized. He said to them: "Bring these images you have found to Ch'oolii (Gobernador Knob), the mountaintop in the center of the world in twelve days." And, with that he disappeared.

On the morning of the appointed day they ascended the mountain on a rainbow provided by the Rainbow People. And, on a level spot near the summit, they met a party that awaited them there. In the group of gods were Hasteyalti, Hastehogan, White Body (who came from the lower world with The People), the eleven divine brothers of Bear Woman, the Mirage Stone People, the Daylight People standing in the East, the Blue Sky People standing in the West and the Darkness People standing in the North.

Hasteyalti laid down a sacred buckskin with its head toward the west. The Mirage Stone People placed on the buckskin, heads to the west, the two little images, of turquoise and white shell, a white and a yellow ear of corn, the Pollen Boy and the Grasshopper Girl. On top of these Hastyalti placed a second sacred buckskin with its head to the east and under this they put Nlch'i (Wind).

Then the gods and the Navajos formed a circle, leaving an opening in the east through which Hasteyalti and Hastehogan went in and out as they sang a sacred song. Four times the gods entered and raised the cover. When they raised it for the fourth time, the images and the ears of corn were found transformed to living beings. The turquoise image had become Estanatlehi, Turquoise, or Changing Woman, and the white shell image had become Yolkai' Estsan, the White Shell Woman. Then the assembly departed, and the two divine sisters Estanatlehi and Yolkai' Estsan were left on the mountain alone.

But in twelve more days, Begochiddi, Black Body, came to First Man and First Woman wanting to see the divine sisters so recently created. They went back to the top of the Mountain in the Center of the World and found that Estanatlehi and Yolkai' Estan were now young maidens. He called to them: "What are your names, daughters?"

He called to them three more times. And on the fourth call, the maidens melded into one beautiful girl. Then, before Begochiddi's eyes, the one maiden changed four times from youth to old age. "This is the Changing Woman," he said. Then, the maiden changed again but remained at an age of about twenty years old. At this point, she began to glow with the iridescence of white shell and Begochiddi said: "You are the White Shell Woman." And with that, they separated and went on about their business.

Begochiddi looked to First Man and First Woman saying: "Mark you the powers of these divine sisters, for they will one day save The People." He left the sisters a basket of beautiful flowers and disappeared into the heavens on a bolt of black lightening.

For an additional four nights the maidens remained there now becoming full-grown women. But on the fourth morning Estsanatlehi said: "Younger sister, why should we remain here? Let us go to yonder high point and look around us."

They went then to the highest point of the mountain. When they had been there several days Estsanatlehi said: "It is lonely here; we have no one to speak to but ourselves; we see nothing but that which rolls brightly over our heads (the sun) and that which drops below us (a small dripping waterfall). I wonder if they can be people? I shall stay here and wait for the one in the morning, while you go down among the rocks and seek the other.''

In the morning Estsanatlehi went to gather wood and wait for the sun as she had told her sister she would do. As she tried to pick up the bundle, she felt something pressing down on it preventing her from lifting it. She became terrified, left the wood bundle and ran home. There, she told White Shell Woman what had happened to her and asked if anything similar had happened at the dripping waterfall.

Yolkai' Estan said that she had merely gone down to collect the water for the day and nothing out of the ordinary happened. So, the sisters decided to do this again. And for three days nothing happened. But on the fourth day, Estanatlehi, again not able to pick up her bundle, found a bare, flat rack and lay on it to rest awhile with her feet to the east. Here, the rising sun shone upon her. She still did not know what had touched her but she was able to take her wood home. Later she would find our that this was the Bearer of the Sun who had fallen in love with her. They separated at this time but would be together in the future.''

Yolkai' Estan went down where the dripping waters descended and allowed them to fall on her. At noon the women met on the mountain top and Estsanatlehi said to her sister: "It is sad to be so lonesome. How can we make people so that we may have others of our kind to talk to?''

Yolkai' Estsan answered: "Think, elder sister, and perhaps after some days you may plan how this is to be done.''

Four days after this conversation, Yolkai' Estsan said:

"Elder sister, I feel something strange moving within me. What can it be?"

Estsanatlehi answered: "It is a child. It was for this that you lay under the waterfall. I feel, too, the motions of a child within me. It was for this that I let the sun shine upon me." Soon afterwards the voice of Hasteyalti was heard to call four times, as usual, and after the last call he and Tonenili (Water Sprinkler) appeared before them. They came to prepare the women for their approaching delivery.

In four more days they felt the commencement of labor and one said to the other: "I think my child is coming." She had scarcely spoken when the voices of Hasteyalti and Tonenili were heard and the gods appeared. The former was the accoucheur of Estsanatlehi and the latter of Yolkai' Estsan. To one woman a drag rope of rainbow was given; to the other a drag rope of sunbeam, and on these they pulled when in pain, as the Navajo woman now pulls on similar ropes. Estsantlehi's child was born first and he, therefore, was the elder brother of Yolkai' Estsan's son and they were to become the Hero Twins.

When the gods returned after four days, the boys had grown to the size of ordinary boys of twelve years. The gods challenged them to a race around a neighboring mountain. Before the race was half done the boys, who ran fast, began to flag; and the gods, who where still fresh, got behind them and scourged the lads with twigs of mountain mahogany. Hasteyalti won the race and the boys came home rubbing their sore backs. When the gods left they promised to return at the end of another four days for another challenge.

As soon as they had gone The Little Winds, who had remained in their ears since their birth, whispered to the boys and told them that the old gods were not all that fast and if the boys would practice during the next four days they might win the coming race. So for four days they ran hard around the mountain, and when the gods returned the boys had grown to the full stature of manhood. In the second race the gods began to flag and fall behind, and the boys got behind their elders and scourged them to increase their speed. The elder of the boys won the race, and when it was over the gods laughed and clapped their hands for they were pleased with the prowess they had witnessed.

The night after they had won the race the boys approached their mothers and asked who their fathers were. "You have no fathers," they were told. "You are illegitimate."

Again the boys demanded: "Who are our fathers?"

The women answered: "The cactus are your fathers."

The next day the women made rude bows of juniper wood and arrows, such as children play with, and said to the boys, "Go and play with these but do not go out of sight of our hut and do not go to the East." Of course the boys were curious and went to the East the first day. When they had traveled a great distance they saw an animal with brownish hair and a sharp nose. They drew their arrows and pointed them toward the strange animal, but before they could shoot he jumped down into a canyon and disappeared. When they returned home they told the women what they had seen. The women said: "That is Coyote which you saw and he is a spy for the alien god, Teelget."

The next day, in spite of warnings not to go out of sight of the lodge, the boys wandered far to the South and there they saw a great black bird seated on a tree. They again aimed their arrows at the strange creature, but again, before they could shoot, the creature disappeared by spreading its wings and flying away. The boys returned to their hogan and said to the women: "Mothers, we have been to the

South today and there we saw a great black bird which we tried to shoot, but before we could let loose our arrows it flew off."

"Alas!" said the women. "It was Raven you saw. He is the spy of Tsenahale, the great winged creature that devours men."

On the third day the boys slipped off and walked toward the West, where they saw a dark bird with a skinny red head that had no feathers on it. This bird they tried to shoot also, but before they could do do it spread its wings and flew away. When they returned home that night they learned that the creature was the Buzzard, the spy for the alien god Tsetahotsiltali (He Who Kicks Men Down the Cliffs).

On the fourth day the boys stole off as usual and went toward the North, where they saw a bird of black plumage perched on a tree on the edge of a canyon. They aimed at this creature, but it also spread its wings and flew away down the canyon. As it flew the boys noticed that its plumes were edged with white. When they returned home they told their mothers, as before, what they had seen. "The bird you saw," said the women, "is the Magpie. He is the spy for the Binaye Ahani, who slay people with their eyes. Alas, our children? What shall we do to make you hear us? What shall we do to save you? You would not listen to us. Now the spies of the alien gods in all quarters of the world have seen you. They will tell their masters and soon the monsters will come here to devour you, as they have devoured all your kind before you."

The next morning the women made a corncake and laid it on the ashes to bake. Then Yolkai' Estsan went out of the hogan and, as she did so, she saw Yeitso, the greatest and fiercest of all the alien gods, approaching. She quickly returned to the hogan and the women hid the boys under bundles and sticks. Yeitso came and sat down at the door just as the women were taking the cake out of the ashes. "That cake is for me," said Yeitso. "How nice it smells."

"No," said Estsanatlehi, "it was not meant for your great mouth."

"I don't care," said Yeitso. "I would rather eat boys. Where are your boys? I have been told you have some here and I have come to eat them."

"We have none," said Estsanatlehi. "All the boys have gone into the paunches of your people long ago."

"No boys?" said the giant. "What, then, made all these little tracks around here?"

"Oh, these tracks I have made for fun," replied the woman. "I am lonely here and I make tracks so that I may fancy that there are many people around me." Then she showed Yeitso how she could make tracks with her fist. He compared these tracks with the ones he had noticed before, seemed to be satisfied and went away.

When he was gone, Yolkai' Estsan, the White Shell Woman, went up to the top of a neighboring hill to look around and from there she saw many of the alien gods approaching in the direction of their hogan. She quickly returned to the lodge and told her sister what she had seen. Estsanatlehi took four colored hoops and threw one toward each of the cardinal points—a white one to the East, a blue one to the South, a yellow one to the West and a black one to the North. At once a great gale arose, blowing so fiercely in all directions from the hogan that none of the monsters could advance against it.

The next morning the boys got up before daybreak and stole away. The women soon missed them but could not trace their tracks in the dark. When it was light enough to examine the ground the women found only four footprints of each boy and these were pointed in the direction of Dzil'na'oodilii (Huerfano Mesa), but more than

eight tracks they could not find. They came to the conclusion that the boys had taken a holy trail, so they gave
up the search and returned to the lodge.

The boys traveled rapidly on the holy trail. (In Navajo
mythology the gods and such men as they favor are
represented in the tales as making a rapid and easy journey
on rainbows, sunbeams and streaks of lightning. Such
miraculous paths are called holy trails.) Soon after sunrise,
they came to a place where they saw smoke arising from
a hole in the ground. They entered the hole by means of
a ladder which projected through it and were welcomed
by an old woman, the Spider Woman. When they reached the floor of Spider Woman's subterranean chamber,
she asked, "Where do you two go walking together?"

"Nowhere in particular," they replied. "We came here
because we have nowhere else to go."

She asked this question four times and each time she
received a similar answer. Then she said: "Perhaps you
seek your father?"

"Yes," they answered, "if we only knew the way to his
dwelling."

"Ah," said the woman, "it is a long and dangerous way
to the house of your father, the Sun. There are many of
the Naye'i dwelling between here and there and perhaps,
when you get there, your father may not be glad to see
you, and may punish you for coming. You must pass four
places of danger: the rocks that crush the traveler, the reeds
that cut him to pieces, the cane cactuses that tear him to
pieces and the boiling sands that overwhelm him. But I
shall give you something to subdue your enemies and
preserve your lives."

Then she gave them a charm which consisted of a hoop
with two life feathers (feathers plucked from a living eagle)
attached and another life feather to preserve their ex-

istence. She also taught them a magic formula, which, if repeated to their enemies, would subdue their anger: "Put your feet down with pollen. (Pollen is the Navajo emblem of peace and this is the equivalent to saying: Put your feet down in peace, etc.)

"Put your hands down with pollen," she said. " Put your head down with pollen. Then your feet are pollen; your hands are pollen; your body is pollen; your mind is pollen; your voice is pollen. The trail is beautiful. Be still." And with that, she sent them on their journey—a journey that would lead to the end of the alien gods and the rebirth of The People.

THE HERO TWINS

Soon after leaving the house of Spider Woman the boys came to a narrow chasm between two high cliffs that were covered with rocks. When a traveler approached, the rocks would open wide, apparently to give him easy passage and invite him to enter. But as soon as he was within the cleft, the rocks would close like hands and crush him to death. These rocks were the Tseyeintili (the rocks that crush) and were alien gods that thought like men. When the boys reached these rocks they lifted their feet as if about to enter the chasm, and the rocks opened to let them in. Then the boys put down their feet, but withdrew them quickly. The rocks closed with a snap but the boys remained safe on the outside. Thus four times did they deceive the rocks. When they had closed for the fourth time, the rocks asked, "Who are you, whence come you two together and wither go you?"

"We are children of the Sun," answered the boys. "We come from Dzil'na'oodilii and we go to seek the house of our father." Then they repeated the words the Spider Woman taught them, and the rocks said: "Pass on to the house of your father, the Sun." When next they stepped into the chasm the rocks did not close and they passed safely on.

They continued on their way until they came to a great plain covered with reeds that had great leaves on them as sharp as knives. When they came to the edge of the field of reeds, the latter opened, showing a clear passage to the other side. They pretended to enter, but quickly retreated, and as they did so the walls of reeds rushed together to kill them. Thus four times did they deceive the reeds. Then the reeds spoke to them, as the rocks had done; they answered and repeated the sacred words. "Pass on to the house of your father, the Sun," said the reeds, and the boys passed on in safety.

Next they came to a country covered with cane cactus. These cactuses rushed at, and tore to pieces, whomever attempted to pass through them. When the boys came the cactuses opened their ranks to let them pass as the reeds had done. But the boys deceived them as they had the reeds and passed safely on.

After they had passed the country of the cactus they reached, in time, the land of the rising sands. Here was a great desert of sands that rose and whirled and boiled like water in a pot, and overwhelmed the traveler that ventured among them. As the boys approached the sands became still more agitated and the boys did not dare venture among them. "Who are you?" asked the sands, "and where do you come from?"

"We are children of the Sun, we came from Dzil'na'oodilii and we go to see the house of our father, the Sun," they answered.

Four times the sands asked and four times the boys answered; then the elder of the boys repeated his sacred formula and the sands subsided, saying, "Pass on to the house of your father, the Sun," and the boys continued on their journey.

Other monsters were encountered and appeased in a like manner before they reached the house of their father. Near Ojo Gallina (the hot springs near San Rafael) they encountered Tieholtsodi, the water monster, whom they appeased with the prayer. Next they came upon Old Age People who treated them kindly but warned them not to follow the trail that leads to the house of Old Age.

They came to Nandz'gai (Daylight) which rose from the ground and let them pass under and then to Chahalgel (Darkness) which also rose and let them pass under. Next they came to Water, which they were able to walk over. They met two bears that growled angrily as if to attack them, a pair of sentinel serpents, a pair of sentinel winds and a pair of sentinel lightnings, all guardians of the dwelling place of the Sun but to all of these the boys repeated the words of the magic formula and were allowed to pass. Finally they met their sister, the daughter of the Sun. She did not speak, but turned silently around and they followed her to the hogan of their father.

The house of the Sun God was built of Turquoise, was square like a pueblo house and stood on the shore of a great water. When the boys entered they saw, sitting in the West, a woman; in the South, two handsome young men (named Black Thunder and Blue Thunder in some versions of the legend); and in the North, two handsome young women. The women gave a glance at the strangers and then looked away. The young men gazed at them more closely and then, without speaking, the women arose, wrapped the strangers in four coverings of the sky and laid them on a shelf.

The boys had lain there quietly for some time when a rattle that hung over the door shook and one of the young women said: "Our father is coming." The rattle shook four times and soon after it had shaken the fourth time, Tsohanoai, the Bearer of the Sun, entered his house. He took the sun off his back and hug it up on a peg on the west wall of the room, where it shook and clanged for some time, going "tla, tla, tla, tla," until at last it hung still.

Then Tsohanoai turned to the women and said in an angry voice: "Who are these two who entered here today?"

The women made no answer and the young people did not look at one another, each fearing to speak. Four times he asked the question and at length the woman said: "It would be well for you not to say too much. Two young men came here today seeking their father. When you go abroad, you always tell me that you visit nowhere, and that you have met no woman but me. Whose sons, then, are these?" she asked, and pointed to the bundle on the shelf. The children smiled significantly at one another.

Tsohanoai took the bundle from the shelf. He first unrolled the robe of dawn with which they were covered, then the robe of blue sky, next the robe of yellow evening light and lastly the robe of darkness. When he unrolled this the boys fell out on the floor. He seized them and threw them first upon great sharp spikes of white shell that stood in the East, but they bounded back, unhurt, from these spikes as they were holding their life-feathers tightly all the while. Next he threw them on spikes of turquoise in the South, on spikes of haliotis in the West and on spikes of black rock in the North, but each time they came back uninjured. Tsohanoai said: "I wish it were indeed true that they were my children."

He said then to the elder children who lived with him: "Go and prepare the sweat house and heat it for four of the hardest boulders you can find. Heat a white, a blue, a yellow and a black boulder." But the Winds heard what he said and knew that he planned to kill his twin sons from earth and made plans to avert their danger.

The sweat house was built against a bank. Wind dug a hole into the bank and concealed the opening with a flat stone. Then he whispered into the ears of the boys and told them about the hole but added that they should not hide in it until they had answered their father's questions. The boys went into the sweat house, the great hot stones were put in, and the opening of the lodge was covered with the four sky blankets. Then Tsohanoai called out to the boys: "Are you hot?" and they answered: "Yes, very hot." Then they crept into the hole Wind had made and hid there. After awhile Tsohanoai came and poured water through the top of the sweat house on the stones, making them burst with a loud noise, and raising a great heat and steam. But in time the stones cooled and the boys crept out of their hiding place into the sweat house. Tsohanoai came and asked again: "Are you hot?" expecting to get no reply, but the boys still answered: "Yes, very hot." Then he took the coverings off the sweat house and let the boys come out. He greeted them in a friendly way and said: "Yes, these are my children," but he was not yet certain and was thinking of other ways in which he might destroy them if they were not.

The four sky blankets were spread on the ground one over another, and the four young men were told to sit on them, one behind another, facing east. "My daughters, make these boys to look like my other sons," ordered their father. The women then pulled the hair of the Hero Twins out long, and molded their faces and forms so that they looked just like their brothers. Then Sun bade them all rise and enter his house. They arose and went, in a procession, the two strangers last.

As they were about to enter the door they heard a voice whispering in their ears: "Psst! Look at the ground." They looked down and saw a spiny caterpillar, who, as they watched, spat out two blue spits on the ground. "Take each of you one of these," whispered Wind, "and put it in your mouth, but do not swallow it. There is one more trial for you, a trial by smoking."

When they entered the house Tsohanoai took down a pipe of turquoise that hung on the eastern wall and filled it with tobacco. "This is the tobacco he kills with," whispered Niltsi to the boys. Tsohanoai held the pipe up to the sun that hung on the wall, lit it, and gave it to the boys to smoke. They smoked it, and passed it from one to another until it was finished. They said it tasted sweet, but it did them no harm.

When Tsohanoai saw that the boys had smoked all of the tobacco and had not been killed by it, he was satisfied and asked: "Now my children, what do you want of me? Why do you seek me?"

"Father," they replied, "the land where we dwell is filled with the Naye'i, who devour the people. There are Yeitso and Teelget, the Tsenahale, the Binaye Ahani and many others. They have eaten nearly all of our kind; there are few left; already they have sought our lives, and we have run away to escape them. Give us, we beg, the weapons with which we may slay our enemies. Help us to destroy them."

"Know," said Tsohanoai, "that Yeitso is also my son, yet I will help you kill him. I shall hurl the first bolt at him and I will give you those things that will help you in war." He took from pegs where they hung around the room and gave to each a hat, a shirt, leggings, moccasins, all made of flint, a chain-lightning arrow, a sheet-lightning arrow, a sunbeam arrow, a rainbow arrow and a great stone knife. "These are what we want," said the boys and put on the clothes of flint and were now dressed exactly like their brothers who dwelt in the house of the Sun.

The next morning Tsohanoai led the boys out to the edge of the world, where the sky and the earth came close together in those times and beyond which there was no world. Here sixteen wands or poles leaned from the earth to the sky, four of which were of white shell, four of which were of turquoise, four of haliotis shell and four of which were of red stone.

"On which wands will you ascend?" Tsohanoai asked his sons. Wind whispered that the red wands were for war, the others for peace, so the boys told their father they wished to ascend on the red ones, for they sought war with their enemies. Along with their father, the boys ascended to the sky on the wands of red stone and they traveled about until Tsohanaoi pointed down and asked: "Where do you belong in the world below? Show me your home."

The brothers looked down and scanned the land but they could distinguish nothing as all the land seemed flat; the wooded mountains looked like dark spots on the surface; the lakes gleamed like stars and the rivers like streaks of lightning. The elder brother said: "I do not recognize the land. I do not know where our home is." At this time Wind prompted the younger brother and showed him which were the sacred mountains and which the great rivers and the younger brother exclaimed, pointing downwards: "There is the Male Water (San Juan River) and there is the Female Water (Rio Grande), yonder is the mountain of Tsisnaajini (Mount Blanca, San Luis Valley, Colorado); below us is Tsoodzil (Mount Taylor, New Mexico) and there in the West is Doko'oosliid (San Francisco Peaks, near Flagstaff, Arizona); that white spot beyond the Male Water is Dibentsaa (Mount Hesperus, Colorado) and between these mountains is Dzilna'oodilii near which our home is."

"You are right, my child, it is thus that the land lies," said Tsohanoai. Then, renewing his promises, he spread a streak of lightning and made his children stand on it, one on each end, and shot them down to the top of Tsood-zil (Mount Taylor). They descended the mountain on its south side and walked toward the warm spring at Tosato (Warm Spring, about three miles south of Grants, New Mexico) where in ancient days there was a much larger lake than there is now. There was a high, rocky wall in the narrow part of the valley and the lake stretched back to where Blue Water is today.

When they came to the edge of the lake, one brother said to the other: "Let us try one of our father's weapons and see what it can do." They shot one of the lightning arrows at Tsoodzil (Warm Spring is about five miles from the base and eighteen miles from the summit of Mount Taylor) and it made a great cleft in the mountain, which remains to this day, and one said to the other: "We cannot suffer in combat while we have such weapons as these."

Soon they heard the sound of thunderous footsteps, for the feet of the monster Yeitso, who lived nearby, stretched as far away as a man could walk between sunrise and noon, and soon they beheld the head of the monster peering over a hill in the east. In a moment he withdrew, and soon afterwards the monster raised his head and chest over a hill in the south, and remained a little longer in sight than when he had in the east. Later he displayed his body to the waist over a hill in the west; and lastly he showed himself, down to the knees, over Tsoodzil. Then he descended the mountain, came to the edge of the lake and put down the basket which he always carried.

Yeitso stooped four times to the lake to drink, and each time he drank the waters perceptibly diminished. When he had done drinking, the lake had nearly drained. As he took his last drink the brothers advanced to the edge of the lake and the monster saw their reflection in the water. He raised his head, and, looking at them, roared: "What a pretty pair have come in sight! Where have I been hunting that I never saw them before?"

"Throw his words back into his mouth," said the younger to the elder brother.

"What a great thing has come in sight! Where have we been hunting that we never saw it before?" shouted the elder brother to the giant.

Four times the taunts were repeated by each party, whereupon the brothers were warned by Wind to take care. They were standing on a bent rainbow just then, which they straightened out. They descended to the ground just as a lightning bolt, hurled by Yeitso, passed thundering over their heads. He hurled four bolts rapidly. As he hurled the second, they bent the rainbow and rose, and it passed under their feet; as he hurled the third they descended and the bolt passed over them, and as he hurled the fourth they again bent the rainbow very high and it passed under their feet and did them no harm. He drew a fifth bolt to throw at them but at this moment the lightning descended from the sky on the head of the giant, causing him to reel. Then the elder brother sped a chain-lightning arrow causing the monster to reel toward the east. The second arrow caused him to stumble toward the south, falling lower. The third lightning arrow made him topple toward the west and the fourth to the north. Then he fell to his knees, raised himself partly again, fell flat on his face, stretched out his limbs and moved no more.

When the arrows struck him, his armor was shivered

in pieces and the scales flew in every direction. The elder brother said, "They may be useful to the people in the future."

The brothers then approached their fallen enemy and the younger scalped him. Heretofore the young brother bore only the name of To'badzistsini, or Child of Water but now his brother gave him also the warrior name of Naidikisi (He Who Cuts Around). Thereafter the elder brother was called Nayenizgani (Slayer of the Alien Gods), or Monster Slayer.

They cut off his head and threw it away to the other side of Tsoodzil, where it still may be seen on the eastern side of the mountain. The blood from the body now flowed in a great stream down the valley, so great that it broke down the rocky wall that bounded the old lake and flowed on. Wind whispered to the brothers that if the blood reached the dwelling of Binaye Ahani, toward which it was flowing, Yeitso would come to life again, so the elder brother took his great knife and drew a line across the valley with it. When the blood reached the line he had made, it stopped flowing and piled itself up in a high wall. But now it began to flow off in the direction of the dwelling place of the alien god, Bear that Pursues, so again the elder hero drew a line with his knife and again the blood piled up and stopped flowing. The blood of the monster Yeitso fills all the valley today, and the high cliffs of black rock that are there now are the places where Nayenezgani stopped the flow with his knife.

Then the Hero Twins put the broken arrows of Yeitso and his scalp into the basket and set out for their home near Dzil'na'oodilii. When they neared the house, they took off their suits of flint armor and hid them, along with the basket and its contents, in the bushes. The mothers were rejoiced to see them and asked where they had been.

"We have been to the house of our father, the Sun," they replied. "And we have been to Tsoodzil and we have slain Yeitso."

"Ah, my child," said Estsanatlehi, "do not speak thus. It is wrong to make fun of such an awful subject."

Then the Hero Twins led their mothers to where they had hidden the basket and showed them the trophies of Yeitso. Changing Woman and White Shell Woman rejoiced and had a dance to celebrate the victory.

"Now," the elder brother asked, "where does Teelget dwell?"

"Seek not to know," his mother replied, "for you have done enough. Rest contented. The land of the alien gods is a dangerous place. They will kill you."

"Yes," the son replied, "and it was hard for you to bear your child, yet you prevailed."

Then Changing Woman told her son where the monster lived, and the next morning he set off to kill him. He came in time, to a great plain, and from one of the small hills that bordered it he saw the monster lying down a long way off. He paused to think how he could approach the monster without attracting its attention, and while he was doing this, Gopher came up to him and said: "I greet you, my friend! Why do you come here?"

"Oh, I am just wandering around," replied the boy.

Four times the question was asked and four times the answer was given, then Gopher said: "I wonder why you came here. No one but I ventures in these parts, for all fear Teelget. There he lies yonder on the plain."

"It is him I seek, but I do not know how to approach him."

"Ah, if that is all you want, I can help you," said Gopher. "And if you slay him, all I ask is his hide. I often go up to him and I will go now to show you." Having said this,

Gopher disappeared in a hole in the ground.

While Gopher was gone the Hero Twin watched Teelget. After a while he saw the great creature rise, walk form the center in four directions, as if watching, and lie down again in the spot where he was first seen. He was a great four-footed beast, with horns like an antelope, as his father was an antelope horn.

Soon Gopher returned and said, "I have dug a tunnel up to Teelget and I have made a hole upward from the tunnel to his heart and four more tunnels in the cardinal directions in which you may hide. I have gnawed the hair off near his heart. When I was gnawing the hair he spoke to me and asked why I was taking his hair, and I replied that I was taking it to make a nest for my children. Then he rose and walked around, but then he came back and lay down where he lay before, over the hole that leads to his heart."

The Hero Twin entered the tunnel and crawled into the end. When he looked up through the ascending shaft of which Gopher had told him, he saw the great heart of Teelget beating there. He sped his arrow of chain lightning and fled into the eastern tunnel. The monster rose, stuck his horns into the tunnel and ripped it open. The Hero Twins fled to the south, the west and the north as the monster followed, but when he had uncovered but half the north tunnel he fell and lay still. Monster Slayer, not knowing that his enemy was dead, and still fearing him, crept back through the long tunnel to the place where he first met Gopher and there he stood gazing at the distant form of Teelget. While he was standing there, he saw a little old man dressed in tight leggings and a tight shirt, with a cap and feather on his head, approaching him. This was Ground Squirrel. "Do you not fear the Naye'i that dwells on yonder plain?"

"I don't know," replied Nayenezgani. "I think I have killed him, but I am not certain."

"Then I shall find out for you," said Ground Squirrel, "for he pays no attention to me. I can approach him any time without danger. If he is dead I will climb upon his horns and dance and sing."

The Hero Twins watched, and before long he saw Ground Squirrel climbing one of the great horns of the monster, dancing and singing.

When Monster Slayer approached his dead enemy he found that Ground Squirrel had streaked his own face with the blood of the slain (and the streaks remain on the ground squirrel's face to this day) and that Gopher had already begun to remove the skin by gnawing on the insides of the forelegs. When Gopher had removed the skin, he put it on his back and said: "I shall wear this in order that, in the days to come when The People increase, they may know what sort of skin Teelget wore." Then Ground Squirrel cut out a piece of the bowel, filled it with the monsters blood, cut off a piece of his liver and gave these to Monster Slayer for his trophies.

He took his trophies home and again there was much rejoicing for another of the alien gods had been destroyed. The Hero Twin remained at home only one day; then he set off to destroy Tsenahale, that monster whose father was a bunch of eagle feathers. He traveled far until he came to a great black rock which looks like a bird, and while he was walking along there, he heard a tremendous rushing sound overhead, like the sound of a whirlwind. Looking up, he saw a creature of great size, something like an eagle in form flying toward him from the East. This creature was the male Tsenahale.

The warrior had barely time to cast himself prone on the ground when Tsenahale swooped over him. Thus four times did the monster swoop at him, coming each time from a different direction. Three times the Hero Twin escaped but the fourth time, flying from the North, the monster seized him in his talons and bore him off to a broad level ledge on the side of a mountain where Tsenshale reared his young. He dropped the Hero Twin on this ledge, as was his custom with all his victims, and perched on a pinnacle above. The fall had killed all the others but the Hero Twin was saved by the life-feather given him by Spider Woman. Then two young of the Naye'i approached to devour the body of the new victim, but he said,"Sh!" at them.

They stopped and cried up to their father: "This thing is not dead! It says 'Sh!' at us."

"That is only air escaping form the body," said the father. "Never mind that. Eat it." Then he flew away in search of other prey.

When the old bird was gone, Monster Slayer hid himself behind the young ones and asked them, "When shall your father return and where will he sit?"

The answered: "He will return when we have a he rain and he will perch on yonder point," indicating a rock close by on the right. Then he asked: "When shall your mother return and where shall she sit?"

They answered: "She will return when we have a she rain and will sit on yonder point," indicating a rock on the left.

He had not waited long when drops of rain began to fall, thunder rolled, lightning flashed, and the male Tsenahale returned and perched on the rock to which the young had pointed. Whereupon Monster Slayer hurled a lightning arrow and the monster tumbled to the foot of Winged Rock, dead.

After awhile rain fell again but there was neither thunder

nor lightning with it. Then there fell upon the ledge the body of a Pueblo woman, covered with fine clothes and ornamented with ear pendants and necklaces of beautiful shells and turquoise. Monster Slayer looked up and saw the female Tsenahale soaring overhead. A moment later she glided down and was just about to light on her favorite crag when Monster Slayer hurled another lightning arrow and sent her body down to the plain to join that of her mate.

The young ones now began to cry and asked the warrior if he would slay them too. "Cease your wailing," he said. "Had you grown up here you would have been things of evil; you would have lived only to destroy my people, but I shall now make of you something that will be of use in days to come when men increase in the land."

He seized the elder and said: "You shall furnish plumes for men to use in their rites, and bones for whistles." He flung the fledgling back and forth four times; as he did so it began to change into a beautiful bird with strong wings, and it said "suk, suk, suk, suk." Then he threw it high in the air. It spread its pinions and soared out of sight, an eagle. To the younger he said: "In the days to come men will listen you your voice to know what will be their future; sometimes you will tell the truth; sometimes you will lie." He swung it back and forth and as he did so its head grew large and round, its eyes grew big and it began to say, "uwu, uwu, uwu, uwu," and it became an owl. Then he threw it into a hole in the side of the cliff and said, "This shall be your home."

Now that his work was done at this place, Monster Slayer decided to return home, but soon discovered there was no way to get down off the ledge. He waited until the sun was about halfway down to the horizon when he observed Bat Woman walking along near the base of the cliff. "Grandmother," he called, "come here and take me down." But she made a sound denoting impatience and contempt and hid behind a rock. Three times she appeared and was asked to take him down and three times she answered in the same way, but when she appeared the fourth time and the Hero Twin asked to be taken down, he added: "I will give you the feathers of the Tsenahale if you will take me off this rock." When she heard this she approached and, after much trouble, took him down in the large carrying basket which she bore on her back.

Together they plucked the two Tsenahale, put the feathers in her basket, and got it on her back. He kept only the largest feather from one wing of each bird for his trophies. As she was starting to leave he warned her not to pass through either of two neighboring localities, which were the dry beds of temporary lakes, one of which was overgrown with weeds, the other with sunflowers. Despite his warning she walked toward the sunflowers. He called after her and begged her not to enter, but she heeded him not and went on.

She had not taken many steps among the sunflowers when she heard a fluttering sound behind her and a little bird of strange appearance flew past close to her ear. At each step she took she heard more fluttering and saw more birds of varying plumage, such as had never been seen before, flying over her shoulders and going off in every direction. She looked around and was astonished to behold that the birds were swarming out of her own basket. She tried to hold them in, to catch them as they flew out, but all in vain. She put down her basket and watched, helplessly, her feathers changing into little birds of all kinds—wrens, warblers, titmice, and the like—and flying away until her basket was empty. Thus it was that the little birds were created.

Monster Slayer returned home with his trophies and the very next day started off to find the alien god known as He Who Kicks People Down the Cliff (Tsetahotsiltali). This Naye'i lived on the side of a high cliff. A trail passed at his feet, and when travellers went that way he kicked them down to the bottom of the precipice. Monster Slayer had not traveled long when he found a well-beaten trail. Following this, he found it led him along the face of a high precipice, and soon he came in sight of his enemy, who had a form much like that of a man. The monster reclined quietly against the rock, as if he meditated no harm, and Monster Slayer advanced as if he feared no danger, yet closely watched his adversary. As he passed, the monster kicked at him, but he dodged the kick and asked: "Why do you kick at me?"

"Oh, my grandchild," said the Naye'i, "I was weary lying thus, and I only stretched out my leg to rest myself." Four times did Nayenezgani pass him and four times did the monster kick at him in vain. Then the hero struck his enemy with his great stone knife over the eyes, and struck him again and again until he was sure he had slain him, but he was surprised to find that the body did not fall down the cliff. He cut with his knife under the corpse in different places, but found nothing that held it to the rock until he came to the head, and then he discovered that the long hair grew, like the roots of a cedar, into a cleft in the rock.

The moment it fell, a great clamor of voices came up from below. "I want the eyes," screamed one. "Give me an arm," cried another. "I want the liver," said a third. "No, the liver shall be mine," yelled a fourth, and thus the quarrelling went on.

Finding a trail that led to the bottom of the cliff, the Hero Twin followed it and soon came upon the young of the Naye'i, twelve in number, who had just devoured their father's corpse. He ran among them, hacking at them in every direction with his stone knife, until he had killed all but one. This one ran faster than the rest and climbed among some high rocks, but Nayenezgani followed and caught him. He saw that the child was disgustingly ugly and filthy. "You ugly thing," said Monster Slayer, "when you ran from me so fleetly I thought you might be something handsome and worth killing, but now that I behold your face I shall let you live. Go to yonder mountain of Naatsis'aan (Navajo Mountain in southeastern Utah) and dwell there. It is a barren land, where you will have to work hard for your living, and will wander ever naked and hungry."

The boy went to Naatisis'aan as he was told, and there he became the progenitor of the Paiutes, a people the old Navajos said were ugly, starved and ragged, who never washed themselves and lived on the vermin of the desert.

The Hero Twin returned home with his trophy, a piece of hair from the Naye'i, and again there was much rejoicing. And, again, the next day he started off in search of others of his enemies, the Binaye Ahani, the people who slay with their eyes. This time, in addition to his other weapons, he carried with him a bag of salt. When he came to the lodge where the alien monsters lived, he entered and sat down on the north side. In other parts of the hogan sat the old couple of the Binaye Ahani and many of their children. They all stared with their great eyes at the intruder, and flashes of lightning streamed from their eyes toward him, but glanced harmlessly off his armor. Seeing that they did not kill him, they stared harder and harder at him, until their eyes protruded far from their sockets. Then he threw the salt into the fire in the center of the lodge, which spluttered and flew in all directions, striking the eyes of the monsters and blinding them. When they held down their heads in pain, he struck with his great stone knife and killed all except the two youngest.

Thus he spoke to the two which he spared: "Had you grown up here, you would have lived only to be things of evil and to destroy men, but now I shall make you of use to my kind in the days to come when men increase on the earth." To the elder he said: "You will ever speak to men and tell them what happens beyond their sight; you will warn them of the approach of enemies," and he changed him into a bird called Tsidildoni (the Screech Owl). Of the younger he made a bird whose duty it was to make the earth happy and the bird is called Hoshdo'il (the Whippoorwill), which is sleepy in the daytime and comes out at night.

When he reached home with the trophies, the eyes of the first Binaye Ahani he had killed, and told what he had done, his mother sang a song about his trophies which would cause the people to be restored.

Next the Hero Twin went out and found Bear that Pursues and killed him. When he had cut off the monster's head, he addressed it, saying: "You were a bad thing in your old life, and tried only to do mischief, but in new shapes I shall make you useful to The People. In the future, when they increase on the earth, you will furnish them with sweet food to eat, with foam to cleanse their bodies and with threads for their clothing." He cut the head into three pieces. He threw one piece to the east, where it became Tsa'zi (Yucca baccata); he threw another to the west, where it became tsasitos (Yucca angustifolia); and he threw the their to the south, where it became the mescal. He cut off the forepaw and took it home for a trophy.

Next the Hero Twin went off in search of Traveling Stone, an alien god who hurled himself at his victims, and found it in the lake which was his home. Traveling Stone hurled itself at Monster Slayer, as if propelled by a giant hand, but the hero raised his lightning arrow, held it in the course of the stone and knocked a piece off the latter. When the stone fell he struck off another piece with his knife.

Traveling Stone now saw it had a powerful foe to contend with, so instead of hurling itself at him again, it fled, and Monster Slayer went in pursuit. He chased it all over the present Navajoland, knocking pieces off it in many places, and at each place where a piece fell there is a constant spring today. Finally he chased it to the San Juan River. Traveling Stone sped down with the current and Monster Slayer ran along the bank after it. Four times he got ahead of the stone, but three times it escaped him by dipping deep into the river. When he headed it off the fourth time, he saw it gleaming like fire under the water and he stopped to gaze at it. Then the stone spoke and said: "Sawe (my baby, my darling), take pity on me, and I shall no longer harm your people, but will do good to them instead. I shall keep the springs in the mountains open and cause your rivers to flow; kill me and your lands will become barren."

The Hero Twin answered: "If you keep this promise I shall spare you, but if you evermore do evil as you have done in the past, I shall seek you again and then I shall not spare you." Traveling Stone kept his promise ever since and has become the Tieholtsodi (Water God) of the upper world.

Now Monster Slayer returned home to rest for four days and give his relatives a full account of his journeys and his adventures from the first to the last.

But still there were many of the Naye'i to be killed. There was White Under the Rock, Blue Under the Rock, Yellow

Under the Rock, Black Under the Rock, and many, many brown giants. Besides these there were a number of stone pueblos, now in ruins, which were inhabited by various animals. During the four days of rest, the brothers talked about how they might slay all of these enemies who filled the land and left no room for The People, and determined to again visit the house of the Sun.

On the morning of the fourth night they started out toward the east. The encountered no enemies on the way and had a pleasant journey. When they entered the house of the Sun, no one greeted them. They sat down on the floor, and as soon as they were seated lightning began to shoot into the lodge. It struck the ground near them four times. Immediately after the last flash Bat and Water Sprinkler entered. "Do not be angry with us," they said. "We flung the lightning only because we feel happy and wanted to play with you."

Still the brothers kept wrathful looks on their faces, until Wind whispered into their ears: "Do not be angry with the strangers. They were once friends of the Naye'i and did not wish them to die, but now they are friends of yours, since you have conquered the greatest of the monsters."

Then, at last, Sun spoke to his children, telling them to be seated, and offered the brothers a seat of shell and a seat of turquoise. But Niltsi whispered in their ears again and told them not to take them as they were seats of peace but to take the seats of red stone—the warrior's seats—instead.

Sun then asked his children why they had come to see him again. Three times he asked the question and three times he was told that his sons had come for no special reason, only to pass away the time. but when he asked them the question the fourth time he demanded that they speak the truth. The elder brother replied: "Father, there are still many of the monsters left, and they are increasing. We wish to destroy them all."

"My children," said Sun, "when I helped you before, I asked you for nothing in return. I am willing to help you again, but I wish to know first if you are willing to do something for me. I have a long way to travel every day, and often, in the long summer days, I do not get through in time, and then I have no place to rest or eat till I get back to my home in the East. I wish you to send your mother to the West that she may make a new home for me there."

"I will do it," said the younger brother. "I will send her there."

But the elder brother said, "No. Changing Woman is under the power of no one. We cannot make promises for her, as she is her own mistress and must speak for herself, but I will tell her of your wishes and plead for you." Then Sun gave his sons five hoops, one black, one blue, one yellow, one white, and a fifth of many colors and shining, and bade them a good day. "Your mother will know what to do with these things," he said.

As they made their way homeward they beheld a beautiful vision. The gods spread out before them the country of the Navajos as it was to be in the future when men increased in the land and became rich and happy.

When the brothers reached home they gave Changing Woman the hoops and told her that their father had said that she would know what to do with them. She replied that she had no knowledge of these talismans of the Sun God as she had never seen him except from afar. But finally she took up the hoops, saying she would see what she could do with them. She took the black hoop, and after spitting the black hail through it, rolled it off to the East. She spat the blue hail through the blue hoop and rolled·

it off to the South, spat the yellow hail through the yellow hoop and rolled it off to the West, and spat the white hail through the white hoop and sped it to the North until it, like the others, was seen no more. Then she threw the hoop of many colors up toward the zenith, and blew a powerful breath after it. Up it went until it was lost to sight in the sky.

For four days nothing happened, but at the end of the fourth day they heard thunder high up in the sky, after which there were four more days of good weather. Then the sky grew dark and a great white cloud descended from above. The cloud was followed by great whirlwinds which uprooted tall trees as if they were weeds and tossed great rocks around as if they were pebbles. For four days and nights a storm of wind and hailed prevailed, such as had never been seen before. When the storm subsided and they came out of their lodge, the air was yet dark and full of dust raised by the high wind, but soon a gentle rain came, laying the dust, and all was clear again.

They marvelled at the sight of the changes the great storm had wrought. Near their house a great canyon had been formed; the bluffs around had been changed and solitary pillars of rock, as one often sees now in Navajoland had been shaped by the winds.

"Surely this stormed killed all the Naye'i," said Changing woman. But Wind whispered in Monster Slayer's ear, "Sa (Old Age) still lives."

The next morning he set out northward, and travelled until he came to a place where he saw an old woman who came slowly toward him leaning on a staff. Her back was bent, her hair was white and her face was deeply wrinkled. He knew this must be Old Age. When they met he said: "Grandmother, I have come on a cruel errand. I have come to slay you."

"Why would you slay me?" she asked in a feeble voice. "I have never harmed anyone. I hear that you have done great deeds in order that men might increase on earth, but if you kill me there will be no increase of men. The boys will not grow up to become fathers, the worthless old men will not die and The People will stand still. It is well that people should grow old and pass away and give their places to the young. Let me live and I shall help increase The People."

"Grandmother, if you keep your promise I shall spare your life," said the Hero Twin, and he returned home without a trophy.

When he reached home Wind whispered: "Hakaz Estsan (Cold Woman) still lives." Again he set out for the North for Cold Woman also lived there, high on the summits where the snow never melts. He traveled to where no trees grew and where the snow lies white all through the summer, and here he found a lean old woman, sitting on the bare snow, without clothing, food, fire, or shelter. She shivered from head to foot, her teeth chattered, and her eyes streamed water. "Grandmother," he said, "a cruel man I shall be. I am going to kill you so that men may no more suffer and die by your hand."

"You may kill me or let me live, as you will. I care not," she said to the hero. "But if you kill me it will always be hot, the land will dry up, the springs will cease to flow, The People will perish. You will do well to let me live. It will be better for your people."

He paused and thought upon her words and decided to let her live.

Again, when he reached home, Wind whispered in his ears saying, "Tgaei (Poverty) still lives."

The next morning he went out and walked until he came upon an old man and an old woman who were filthy, clad in tattered garments, and had no goods in their house. "Grandmother, grandfather," he said, "a cruel man I shall be. I have come to kill you."

"Do not kill us, my grandchild," said the old man. "It would not be well for The People, in the days to come, if we were dead. Then they would always wear the same clothes and never get anything new. If we live the clothing will wear out and the people will make new and beautiful garments and they will gather goods and look handsome. Let us live and we will pull their old clothes to pieces for them." So he spared them and went home.

The next journey was to seek our Dichin (Hunger). He journeyed until he came upon twelve of the Hunger People. Their chief was a big, fat man, although he had no food to eat but the little brown cactus. "I am going to be cruel," the hero said, "so that men may suffer no more the pangs of hunger and die no more of it."

"Do not kill us," said the chief, "if you wish your people to increase and be happy in the days to come. We are your friends. If we die people will not care for food and they will never know the pleasure of cooking and eating nice things, and they will never care for the pleasures of the chase." So he spared Hunger and went home.

When the Hero Twin reached home Wind spoke to him no more of enemies that lived. The Slayer of the Alien Gods said to his mother, "I think all the Naye'i must be dead, for every one I meet now speaks to me as a relation; they say to me, 'my grandson,' 'my son,' 'my brother.'" Then he took off his armor and put it away with the weapons the Sun had given him, and sang a song.

When he had finished the song, his father visited him and took away the armor and trophies, saying, "These I shall carry back to my house in the East and keep them safe. If you ever need them again, come and get them."

Then he promised to return in four days and meet Changing Woman on the top of Ch'oolii (Gobernador Knob) and left.

At the end of four days Changing Woman went to the top of Ch'oolii and met the Sun, who asked her to come away and make a home for him in the West. She agreed on the condition that he would build her a house as beautiful as the one he had in the East, which her sons had told her about. "I want it built floating on the western water," she said, "away from the shore so that in the future, when people increase, they will not annoy me with too many visits. I want all sorts of gems—white shell, turquoise, haliotis, jet, soapstone, agate, and redstone—planted around my house, so that they will grow and increase. Then I shall be lonely over there and shall want something to do, for my sons and my sister will not go with me. Give me animals to take along. Do all this for me and I shall go with you to the West." He promised all these things to her, and he made elk, buffalo, deer, long-tail deer, mountain sheep, jackrabbits and prairie dogs to go with her.

When she started for her new home twelve of the divine people went with her to help her drive her animals, which were already numerous and increasing daily. At Black Mountain the buffaloes broke from the herd and ran to the East; they never returned and are in the East still. Sometime later the elks went to the East and they never returned. From time to time a few of the antelope, deer and other animals of the herd left and wandered East. After a while Changing Woman arrived at the great water in the West and went to dwell in her floating house beyond the shore. Here she still lives, and here the Sun visits her, when his journey is done, every day that he crosses the sky.

When Changing Woman had departed, her sons went, as their father had bidden them, to the valley of the San Juan River where they made their dwelling. They are there to this day and the Navajos still go there to pray for success in war, but only warriors go.

HOW THE PEOPLE CAME TO BE AGAIN

The myth tales are somewhat vague as to whether there were any earth surface people left after the Naye'i got through with their rampage. Well, more than "somewhat vague." The subject is just never mentioned and the only time I had an opportunity—and got up the nerve—to ask anyone who was in a position to know, the reply to my question was a thoughtful stare at spot just above my head and this answer: "That's up to you."

No, I was not being told it was being left up to me to put people on earth at that time (in my mind) if that was what I wanted. Yet, in a very Navajo way, I was being told exactly that, along with several other things, all expressed in those four simple words.

Many traditional Navajo people have a wonderful way of communicating precisely what they intend by avoiding directly expressing it in words. As Shirley Sells once put it, "sometimes the briefest of eye contact says it all." And sometimes they will stare at a spot somewhere just above your head and, seemingly, change the subject entirely. What follows is an exact exchange I once heard. Some sort of semi-uniformed official, perhaps governmental and perhaps merely self-appointed (you find a lot of those around Indian reservations), walked up to an old woman who was watching her daughter-birthed-by-her-sister (in the Navajo kinship system, the children of a woman's sister are considered as closely related as the children to whom she gave birth) weave in the shade of of a bush shelter. He had already played loose with a couple of serious social taboos, even before he opened his mouth.

"Hot one, huh? Lot of sheep over there," he nodded toward a flock of about thirty sheep standing in the shade about fifty yards away. "All them sheep belong to you, Auntie?"

Auntie?

"Auntie" Grandmother Begay glanced at my new silver and turquoise bracelet she'd just been admiring, as if checking to see if it was still there. Then at a spot just over The Uniform's head. "They say they got lots of drunk people in Gallup," she said quietly. And extremely politely, too.

In my mind and also in that of her daughter who allowed the beginning of a smile to play at the corner of her mouth, she'd made her point. However, The Uniform went away thinking, for all the world, he'd just tried to be friendly to one more crazy old Navajo woman.

Back to the subject of Alien Gods and people. I really don't know if the Naye'i ate all the Navajos that existed before Changing Woman. I do know they didn't eat all the Kisani because there is a myth tale that mentions a few Pueblos running loose afterwards (no, all the myth tales are not told or mentioned in this short work; one could easily fill a volume ten times this size and still have material left over for a large book of Coyote tales). Anyway, Changing Woman and White Shell Woman had to create more to replace those who'd been destroyed by the Naye'i. And with the new people, the complicated Navajo clan and kinship systems came into being.

What happened to Monster Slayer and Born of Water? Like so many Navajo gods, they went off to the east to live with Daylight. The Sun Bearer promised them he'd return their weapons to them if they were ever needed again to save the Navajo people from Monsters. I know a few Navajos who think it is high time Sun Bearer kept his promise. In the last few years that monster, Poverty, has gotten totally out of hand.

THE PEOPLE GATHER

Changing Woman's younger sister, White Shell Woman, started out with the Hero Twin brothers but when they stopped to build their dwelling at Toyetli, where the San Juan is joined by a second sacred stream she went on, alone, to the San Juan Mountains as that was where The People had come from long before. There, on the shores of the lake that was home to the island that was the Place of Emergence, she built a good hogan for herself.

She swept the floor clean and made a comfortable bed of soft grass and leaves for herself but she was terribly lonely and could not sleep. She lay awake wandering how some people to keep her company might be created.

Four days after she had constructed her hut, she was visited by Hasteyalti, Talking God, who announced his approach with his usual call of "hu, hu, hu, hu."

"Where were you, my granddaughter, that you saved yourself from the alien gods when the were eating the earth surface people?"

"I was at Dzil Na'oodili with my sister. Now, however,

I am alone in these mountains. I have been hoping there might be some people to relieve my great loneliness. Where do you come from, my grandfather?"

"I come from the mountain in the east where the gods dwell. And I take pity on you in your loneliness and wish to help you. Remain here and I shall return in four days".

At dawn on the fourth day after Hasteyalti took his leave, White Shell Woman again heard the "hu hu hu hu" call that signaled his presence.

Then she heard the sound of another voice calling, and that was the voice of Hastehogan, the House God. They were accompanied by numerous divine ones, including those gods of the sacred mountains who formed themselves in a circle in front of White Shell Woman's hogan, which would have been to the east, of course. They all stood in the direction assigned to the mountains to which they belonged, hence Rock Crystal Boy and Rock Crystal Girl, the male and female gods of Tsisnaajini (Blanca Peak) stood in the east; Boy Who Carries One Turquoise and Girl Who Carries One Turquoise and belong to Tsoodzil (Mount Taylor) stood in the south, as that was their direction, and so on until all the sacred mountain gods were in their proper place.

And thus they stood during the ceremony that followed, which was the same as the corn ceremony by which First Man and First Woman were created, and again the white ear of corn was changed into a man and the yellow ear of corn was changed into a woman and these were given the breath of life by Wind. When Hastseyalti threw the sacred top buckskin off the new pair, a dark cloud descended and covered their forms like a blanket. White Shell Woman led them into her hogan and the assembled gods dispersed, but before he left, Hastseyalti promised to return in four days.

Early on the fourth day after his departure, Hasteyalti returned to White Shell Woman's hogan and brought with him Mirage Boy and Ground Heat Girl.

Then he gave her two ears of corn saying, "Grind only one grain at a time," and departed. White Shell Woman said to the newly arrived couple: "This boy and girl of corn cannot marry one another for they are brother and sister, and neither can you marry each other because you are also brother and sister. Yet I must do something for you all."

So she married the boy made of corn to the Ground Heat Girl and the girl made of corn to the Mirage Boy, and soon each couple had two children, a boy and a girl. When these children were old enough to travel, they moved away from there and moved to White Standing Rock and from these people are descended the clan called House of Dark Cliffs (Note: Or so it was recorded by Washington Matthews. I've been told that this was actually the Anasazi descended clan, Towering House. As there seems to be some doubt about the names of the clans that came about after White Shell Woman, I'm not using the disputed names here.) Thirteen years passed and they saw no sign of existence of any people but themselves until one night they saw the gleam of a distant fire. For four days and four nights they sought out the fire but could not find it until Wind whispered, "The fire shines through a crack in the mountain. Cross the ridge and you will find the fire."

They had not gone far over the ridge when they saw the footprints of men, then the footprints of children, and soon they came to a camp. One party was as much rejoiced as the other to find people like themselves in the wilderness. They embraced one another and shouted mutual greetings and questions. The new people said they had come from a poor land where they had lived on ducks and snakes. The new party consisted of twelve persons, five men, three women, one grown girl, one grown boy and two small children. The place where the strangers were encamped was called Bend in a Canyon, and they were the ancestors of another clan.

Soon afterwards White Shell Woman left The People and went to dwell forever in the San Juan Mountains in a house of White Shell which had been prepared for her. But she still comes to visit the Navajos in the female rain for she is ever present in the soft rains.

Fourteen years later The People were joined by another people who had come from Huerfano Mesa and seven years later a fourth clan joined them. The new arrivals said they had been seeking The People all over the land for many years. Sometimes they would come upon the remains of old camps and again they would find deserted brush shelters, partly green or, again, quite green and fresh. Occasionally they would observe faint footprints and think they were just about to meet another people like themselves in the desolate land, but again all traces of humanity would be lost. They were rejoiced to meet at last The People they had so long sought. The new people camped close to the people from Huerfano Mesa and discovered that they and the latter carried similar red arrow-holders, such as the other clans did not have, and this led.hem to believe they were related.

Fourteen years later, the Navajos moved to Chaco Canyon. They camped at night in a scattered fashion and made so many fires that they attracted the attention of some strangers camped on a distant mountain, and these strangers came down and they too were a similar people and joined the tribe. It was autumn when the fifth clan arrived. Then all The People moved to the banks of the San Juan River, where they built warm huts for winter.

All the fall and winter, when the days were fair, they worked in the bottom lands grubbing up roots and getting the soil ready for gardens to be planted in the spring.

When The People had been living on the banks of the San Juan for six years a new band joined them. As yet The People had no horses, domestic sheep or goats. They rarely succeeded in killing a deer or Rocky Mountain sheep. When they secured deer it was sometimes by still-hunting them, sometimes by surrounding one and making it run until it was exhausted, and sometimes by driving them over precipices. When a man got two skins of these larger animals he made a garment of them by tying the forelegs together over his shoulders. The women, in those days, wore a garment consisting of two webs of woven cedar bark, one hanging in front and one behind. Everyone wore sandals of yucca fiber or cedar bark. Their blankets were made of cedar bark, of yucca fiber, or of skins sewed together. Each house had, in front of the door, a long passageway in which hung two curtains, one at the outer, the other at the inner end, usually made of woven cedar bark. In winter they brought in plenty of wood at night, closed both curtains, and made the house warm before they went to sleep. Their bows were of plain wood as the Navajos had not yet learned to put animal fiber of the backs of the bows. Their arrows were mostly of reeds tipped with wood. The land which they farmed was surrounded by high bluffs.

After a time The People became too numerous for all of them to dwell where they were, so some went up on the bluffs to live and built stone storehouses in the cliffs, and others moved across the San Juan and raised crops on the other side of the stream.

In the next two decades The People were joined by three other bands of Navajos, the third of which was very numerous and came from the White Valley among the Waters, which is near where the city of Santa Fe now stands. These people had long viewed in the western distance the mountains where The People dwelt, wondering if anyone lived there and, at length, set out to see. They journeyed westward twelve days until they reached the mountains and spent eight days traveling among them before they encountered The People. The people of this new clan were good hunters and very skilled in making weapons and beautiful buckskin shirts and they taught their arts to the other clans.

Now at this time The People still lived about the valley of the San Juan, remaining in one place both summer and winter as the Navajos did not become wanderes until they got the sheep. But The People became so numerous that the men had to go farther and farther away to hunt, and on their journeys they encountered many people—some of whom were like the Navajos and spoke the same or a similar language. And many of these people came to live among The People and new clans were added in this manner.

A number of Utes visited the Navajos there once. They came when the corn ears were small and remained till the corn was harvested. They worked for the Navajos, and when their stomachs were filled, all left except for one family, which consisted of an old couple, two girls and a boy. These at first intended to stay only a short time after their friends had gone, but they tarried longer and longer until they ended up joining with the Navajos. One of the girls, whose name was Sage Brush Hill, lived to be an old woman and the mother of many children, and from her is descended the clan of Sage Brush Hill.

Some years later a large band of Apaches from the South came to the settlement on the San Juan and told the Navajos that they had left their old tribe forever and desired to become Navajos. They all belonged to one clan among the Apaches and were taken in by the Navajos as the new clan, Naashgali Dineh (Mescalero Apache clan)

About this time there was a famine in Zuni and some people from that pueblo came and were admitted into the tribe, but they were not formed into a new clan but were added to an existing one. The Zuni clan was formed much later.

More and more, bands of Navajos came among The People on the San Juan and were admitted as clans, as well as the people from an old pueblo named Tlogi which was near where Jemez now stands. These people, who were starving, formed the clan of Tlogi (the Weaver Clan).

Before this time the Navajos had been a weak and peaceful tribe, but now they found themselves becoming a numerous people and they began to talk of going to war. Of late years they had heard much of the great pueblos along the Rio Grande, but how those people had saved themselves from the Naye'i the Navajos did not know. A man named Napailinta got up a war party and made a raid on Red House pueblo and returned with some captives, among whom was a girl, and from her is descended Red House (Kin Lichiini) clan.

The captives from Red House were, at first, slaves among the Navajos, but their descendants became free and increased greatly and from them came the clan of Tlizi Lani (Many Goats).

In this way the Navajo people grew in number and their power increased. It was about this time the people from the shores of the great water in the West came to join the Navajos.

One night two strange men entered the Navajo camp. They spoke the Navajo language and told The People they were the advance couriers of a multitude of wanderers who a had left the shores of the great waters in the West to join the Navajos along the San Juan river, of whom they had heard. The ancestors of these people were made by Changing Woman, who became lonely in her hogan made of turquoise for her in the Western sea, and created them for company.

This is how that came about. Sun Bearer kept his promise and built for her the hogan that was an exact duplicate of his own hogan in the east that the Hero Twins had visited and described to their mother. However, Sun Bearer was always busy during the time of light because had he not been in the sky there would have been no light. She grew tired of this state of affairs and took it upon herself to make some new people.

When she had made these people from the skin from under her left arm, from the skin under her right arm, and from other parts of her body, she said to these people: "I wish you to dwell near me, where I can always see you, but if one day you choose to go east to where your kindred dwell, you may go."

When these people had lived on the shore of the great water for many years, some of them went to Changing Woman and told her that they wished to go and live among their kindred in the East as the People were few where they lived and had many enemies, and they felt that they would be better off where there were more of their kind.

On the appointed day they set out on their journey to the East, and after they had traveled for twelve days they crossed a high ridge and came in sight of a great treeless plain, in the center of which they observed some dark objects in motion. They continued on but tried to avoid the dark objects, which they suspected of being men, by keeping among the foothills and under the cover of the timber that surrounded the plain. As they went along they could see the dark objects more plainly and discovered that these were indeed human beings.

In spite of the precautions taken by the travelers, they had been seen by the people of the plain, and when they camped at night two of the latter visited them. The visitors said they were the Kiltsoi and the plain in which they lived was extensive, and that they had water melons getting ripe, with corn and other food in their gardens. The travelers decided to remain with these people for a while.

The second night two more visitors came into the camp and one of them fell in love with a maiden of the Western people and stayed with her in the camp as long as her people remained in the valley, except for the last two nights when she went and stayed with his people. These Kiltsoi gave the wanderers an abundance of the produce of their fields and they, of course, fared well. When the travelers were prepared to move on, they implored the young husband to go with them. He wanted his wife to stay there, among his people, but in the end the woman's relations prevailed and the Kiltsoi man joined them on their journey. In the meantime four other men of the Kiltsoi had fallen in love with maidens of the wanderers and these enamored young men also joined the travelers.

As these people continued on their journey east, they encountered many difficulties, for they soon came to a land in which they could find no water. For five days they walked across a parched wasteland before finding water in a hole: A woman was the first to taste it. "It is bitter water," she cried. "Let that be your name and the name of your people," one who had heard her said, and thus did the clan of the Bitter Water People receive its name. A few days later another woman found some water but it was salty, and from her is descended the Salt Clan.

The wanderers traveled steadily for thirty-one days after leaving the Kiltsoi, until they reached the San Francisco mountains. Here they stopped for several days to rest and built a stone wall around their camp, which still stands. When they again resumed their journey they were forced to travel much slower as there was little food and the men had constantly to stop and hunt.

It was late autumn when they stopped to rest the second time, and this is where these people from the West became divided into two parties. One group wanted to remain where they were, in hopes that some of their kindred people, whom they knew must be somewhere nearby, would find them. The second group wanted to push on and find the kindred people themselves, so they left. But soon after they had gone, those who remained in the camp sent out two messengers, and later they sent out two more, to induce their people to come back to the camp. The first two couriers, searching for these people, came to a place where the runaways had divided into two bands, one of which travelled east and it is from this group that the Jicarilla Apaches are descended. The other band wandered off to the North and became those kindred tribes who live far to the North (Canada and Alaska) who speak a language much like the Navajo.

The second pair of messengers pursued this band, traveling north for a great distance, but finally gave up the task and returned to the camp. The first pair followed the band traveling east but soon despaired of overtaking these people and turned south toward the San Juan River, where they found the Navajos Changing woman had told them about. These two messengers were the men of whom you have heard before, who entered the camp of the Navajos and told of the coming of the people from the West.

The wanderers stayed in their camp all that winter, but with the coming of spring they resumed their journey. Along the way, for one reason or another, groups of them stopped to remain at places they found favorable. One group stopped to live at a place where a great lone tree stood and these people became the clan called Tsin Sikaadnii (Clumped Tree) Other groups stopped here and there and often became new clans named after some landmark nearby. However, man of the wanderers continued on and soon joined their kinsmen on the San Juan River.

As the years passed several bands of Apaches joined the Navajos on the San Juan River and became clans. Then another party of Zuni Indians were taken into the tribe, and a new people with painted faces who came from the West and are supposed to have been Mohaves were also adopted into the tribe.

In this manner all of the old clans of the Navajo were formed and all this happened long ago, before the Spaniards came into the land. Later some Utes raided far to the South and captured a Spanish woman, whom they sold to the Navajos, and from her is descended the clan of the White Stranger People, or Mexican People (Naakaii Dineh) clan. During the Pueblo wars with the Spaniards many fugitives came among the Navajo to live, and from the women of these people are descended still other clans, such as the Naashashi (Bear Enemy, or Tewa) Clan.

And it has always been told that this is the manner in which the Navajos got together.

SPIDER WOMAN

Spider woman instructed the Navajo women how to weave on a loom which Spider Man told them how to make. The cross poles were made of sky and earth cords, the warp sticks were made of sun rays, the healds of rock crystal and sheet lightning. The batten was a sun halo, white shell made the comb. There were four spindles; one a stick of zigzag lightning with a whorl of channel coal; one a stick of flash lightning with a whorl of turquoise; a third had a stick of sheet lightning with a whorl of abalone; a rain streamer formed the stick of the fourth and its whorl was a white shell." Or so we are told in one myth tale about Spider Woman. Short tales of Spider Woman crop up throughout Navajo mythology.

She always lives in a hole in the ground with one exception that I know of: the Spider Woman of Canyon de Chelly lives atop the split tower called Spider Rock which is about five miles east of the mouth of the canyon on the south rim. Nowadays, there is a good blacktop road, a well-marked turnout, a parking lot, guardrails and the whole nine yards. The last time I was there, in 1987, there was a bone rattling wind, it was spitting snow, sleet, hail, and still the sun was trying to come out. I was with Christopher Riccella and we were both fascinated by the grandeur of that incredibly beautiful place, seemingly with not another soul within miles—and trying to get a photograph of Spider Rock illuminated by a sun ray.

Not many people have every seen Canyon de Chelly and Spider Rock under more than a foot of fresh snow. Certainly not a lot of people who have to drive a Honda to get there and have any sense at all, haven't. The road along the south rim has been paved only a few years. Used to be you had to drive a dirt road up past an ancient deserted hogan with a hole in the north wall indicating a dead body had been removed when the hogan was abandoned. Then you took the next goat path off to the left and stumbled down some gullies. You came up to the top of a little hill and there is was, all spread out in front of you with Spider Rock in the foreground. And about twenty feet down that little hill was a very sudden nearly two thousand foot drop to the bottom of the canyon. It was a little frightening. Once I went there with a party that included a man from England who was terrified of heights. One glance down that slab of sandstone and he was frightened witless. It took him several hours to regain control of his shaking hands.

The sun finally did throw a slash across Spider Rock and we got some beautiful photographs, as it turned out. It was worth being snowed in to see the "Cathedral of the Navajos" under all that new snow, with sun and shadows weaving back and forth. Then something happened that made that day very special. On the wind, from not too far away, came the voice of a Navajo man, out riding alone, singing a song to his horse. His voice was strong and clear, and the wind and the deep canyon walls threw it back to us. The song went on for ten or fifteen minutes.

The Spider Woman who is supposed to live atop Spider Rock? I've been told that it's rumored she kidnaps badly behaved children, eats them and throws the bones over the side. I have also been told that she's not the Navajo Spider Woman; that she really belongs to the Hopi who, a couple of hundred years ago, had farms on the Canyon floor.

There are several Spider Woman stories. And Spider Man is also the subject of several tales. The one that follows is my favorite.

SPIDER WOMAN STORY

Old Navajos say, long ago at Blue House in the time before the Great Gambler, near Kintyel, there was a Kisani woman who was so ugly that nobody wanted her—not even her relatives. Her father and mother were dead, so she went from hogan to hogan of the Navajos to earn her living by grinding corn and cooking. No man seemed to want her for a wife, so she had no choice but to wander from place to place looking for a way in which to feed herself.

One morning she went out to pick some berries, but she was gone all day and filled only the smallest of the four baskets she carried with herself. She camped out that night, sleeping in the ruins of one of those old stone house ruins the Kisani built when they first arrived in the Fifth World. That tells you how desperate this woman was because most people would know better than disturb such a place. Early the second morning she started walking to the north and east towards Kinnebito. She had been told that some relatives of her mother lived over that way and she thought she'd look into this matter.

Near the path up there among some rocks, she saw smoke rising up from the ground. "I wonder what that could be?" she asked herself, and decided to go there in search of food and warmth. To her surprise, when she reached her destination she found that the smoke was rising from the bottom of a little round hole. Waving the smoke away, she was able to look inside the hole. And much to her amazement she saw an strange looking old woman who was every bit as ugly as she was sitting by the warmth of the fire spinning a web. It was the Spider Woman, and when she saw a shadow over the hole she looked up and saw the Kisani woman staring down at her.

"Do not be afraid, my daughter. Come down into my house and visit with me," the old woman said.

"The hole is much too small for me to enter," replied the Kisani woman.

"It is big enough," replied the Spider Woman.

Then she blew her breath up the hole four times and it opened out bigger and bigger until it became a wide passageway, with four ladders leading up to the top. On the east was a white ladder, on the south a blue one, on the west a yellow one, and on the north a black one.

The Kisani woman climbed down the blue ladder into the abode of the Spider Woman who was weaving something. "Come down and sit here beside me and watch what I do, my grandchild," the old woman said. And the Kisani woman did as she asked.

The Spider Woman was using a stick about a foot long with a hole in one end like a needle, and with this she passed the thread in and out, making a blanket. "What is this that you do, grandmother?" the Kisani girl asked.

"It is a blanket I weave," the old woman replied.

"Does it have a name, my grandmother?"

"I will name it Black Design Blanket." And this became the Black Design Blanket, the first blanket of the Navajo.

After Spider Woman had finished what she was weaving, she went up to the top of the ground and, throwing her web up, she caught the sun and coaxing it with a "suk, suk," she pulled the Sun farther to the west and came back.

"How quickly the time passes," she said and returned to her loom. Soon she went up again and pulled the Sun lower until it was almost sunset. This the Kisani girl watched the old woman do four times in all. Then Spider Woman told the girl the Sun was low and it would soon be dark.

"It is late and I must be leaving," the girl said.

"Please. Spend the night with me, my grandchild." This the Kisani woman agreed to and began to settle for the night.

Just then Spider Man came down into the hole.

"Where is this earth surface woman from?" he asked. "And what is she doing here?"

"They were mean to our grandchild up there and treated her badly," said his wife. "That is why she goes around picking up things to get a living."

Spider Woman made some dumplings out of grass seeds and fed the girl and the next morning started weaving another blanket. She worked so fast that she finished it that day. It was square and as long as her arm and she named this new blanket Pretty Design Blanket. The girl watched her all day and stayed there a second night, and the following morning the Spider Woman started still another blanket. She finished this blanket, which she called White Striped Blanket, that day, and on the fourth morning she began another. This was a "Beautiful Design Skirt" such as Yeibichai dancers and Snake dancers wear, and was white with figures in black.

The next morning the Kisani girl went back to the hogan where she had been staying and asked the Navajos for some cotton in three colors—yellow, black, and white. After the cotton had been given to her, she put up a loom, but not like the Spider Woman's loom. She put it up the way Navajo women do now and began a blanket. Her blanket was about half done when another Kisani woman came in and looked at the loom and the design. The girl had made a picture of a bird on both sides of the blanket.

"Where did you learn to do that?" the Kisani woman asked. "I did this on my own thought," answered the girl. "It is called a Black Design Blanket."

She finished it in one day, and the next morning she put up her loom again and asked for more cotton to weave. She made a Beautiful Design Skirt the same day. It was finished when two Kisani men came to see what she was doing and asked to see the blankets she had made. One examined the Beautiful Design Blanket very carefully. The second man observed the Black Design weaving. They then returned to their homes and made looms, copying the designs they had learned. And this is why it is the Kisani men who are known for their beautiful weaving.

The girl only made two blankets and then went back to Spider Woman's house. Spider Woman was now weaving a wicker water jar and after that she wove a big carrying basket such as Navajo women used to carry on their backs. The Kisani girl learned to make the basket and then the water jar. "When I went back," she told Spider Woman, "I showed the people how to make blankets like yours. Now I will go back and make carrying baskets and water jars."

"That is good," said Spider Woman. "I am glad you have taught them. But whenever you make a blanket, you must leave a hole in the middle the way I do. For if you do not, your weaving thoughts will be trapped within the cotton and not only will it bring you bad luck, but it will drive you mad."

The girl went back to her hogan and made a carrying basket and a water jar.

"Where do you learn all these things?" The People asked.

"I just guessed it out," she said.

The Navajo women watched her, and soon they were all making carrying baskets and then they learned to make water jars and blankets too, just like those of the Spider Woman. Unlike the Kisani men, it is the Navaho women who kept on with their blanket weaving. And they always left the spider-hole in the middle of each blanket, like the hole in the center of a spider web. That keeps them from getting "blanket sickness" of the mind from keeping the weaving patterns inside their heads. Navajo women almost never draw their blanket patterns down but keep them inside as Spider Woman did.

And that's true, even today.

THE MAN WHO KILLED SANTA CLAUS

How long does a story have to be around to be considered a "folktale?" I don't really know if the story of the man who killed Santa Claus would make the cut for some people.

Perhaps it is too modern. There are many such; one about Coyote losing his tail—and subsequently his head—down near Lupton; another about a ghost up near Shiprock (that one never sounded very Navajo to me), and the two I've chosen to tell here—in condensed form—are among them. Whatever a folktale is, to paraphrase a famous statement, I know one when I hear it. Ralph Weinstock once put it about as well as it can be said: "There is magic in folktale, magic in hearing a folktale for the first time, and a magic in telling it again."

I first heard the story of the man who killed Santa Claus the first fall I spent in Navajoland, over twenty years ago. It had the magic because the man who told it to me was magical. His name was Manuelito Begay and, like many Navajo people, if he took a liking to you, it was immediate and he was your friend forever. He was a Navajo Singer, a very spiritual man and this is how I met him.

My interest in Native Americans had, up until I met Manuelito Begay—we can begin this journey rather specifically in August, 1968—had been directed more toward the Zuni and the Pueblo peoples of the Rio Grande.

One day, I was driving to Los Angeles from Santa Fe and my wonderful new German automobile broke down. I didn't know it but I was somewhere between Lupton and Chambers, Arizona. On the Navajo Reservation.

First this wonderful little machine from Germany started spewing a lot of white smoke from somewhere in front—in the general area of the motor. The last thing I'd seen that resembled a garage had been back across the New Mexico state line near Gallup. So much smoke was pouring out of this vehicle—and directly onto the windshield—that I could barely see to keep it on the pavement. I took the first exit—one that I was to see many times in the future and the sight of which would cause me to make a hasty and unwise decision in the middle of the worst storm of the winter of 1987.

That led me to a tumbledown one pump gas station. By this time my new car was making some rather weird sounds. A young Navajo man came out of the garage and stood staring at the smoke. He was smiling. First lesson: If a Navajo smiles at a stranger, the joke is not on the Navajo.

"Hmmmm," said the mechanic who, I would soon learn, was called Billie Begay. "Goes hump, hump."

"Yes," I agreed. But it seemed to me it was supposed to go whir, whir.

He smiled some more. An old man seated over against the wall who'd been ignoring me, my smoking car and all other activity as far as I could tell, apparently grew bored, aroused himself and came to take a look as Billie

Begay lifted the hood and said, "Hmmmmm. A lot of smoke. Smells of oil."

It surely did. He smiled. The old man smiled. I saw nothing to smile about and certainly not after getting Billie Begay's summation of my situation. I had thrown a rod. There was not a Mercedes dealer within two hundred miles. But there was a fellow back in Gallup, only thirty miles or so away who worked on foreign cars. Especially, as it turned out, ones that broke down on the way to California.

Another Navajo man interrupted to buy diesel fuel which was sold to him out of a drum.

No, there was not a telephone there I could use to call this man who worked on California bound foreign cars, not there, nor did anyplace nearby have a phone. But Billie Begay would be only too happy to drive me into Gallup at closing time, as he was going there anyway and knew where the foreign auto man lived. He even knew his name but considering how much ransom he eventually held my automobile for, I'm sure his descendants will be eternally grateful if I don't reveal it. Later one of them, a son, became a friend.

Well, it was either that or hitchhike, the sun was hot, the wind was fierce and blowing large insects about like miniature kamikaze bombers. And it was only three hours to closing time. I decided I'd purchase a bottle of Billie Begay's hot orange pop ("No CoCola," he said, frowning slightly about the mouth). And complain about the heat and insects until Billy Begay got through with work. Which was not at "closing time" but precisely when Billie Begay decided it was time to do so. Lesson number two in Navajo social behavior.

The passing of time was marked by Billie Begay's cursing the old Ford pickup he was working on. He'd picked up quite a gift for English swear words with which he liberally sprinkled his Navajo. The effect was sort of startling. Something like "Goddam ajilchi, achaiya, dahazho ma'ike nagha sumbitch!" An hour passed, during which the old man barely moved. At times I wondered if he was breathing. Yet, when I wasn't looking at him I got the feeling he was looking at me.

"He's got some women troubles in Gallup," the old man said, so quietly I barely heard the words.

"Huh?"

Without looking at me, he nodded his head toward Billie, "Women troubles in Gallup."

"I see."

"He'll hurry. Take you."

That was reassuring but not the fist size grasshopper that flew into my face. I cursed that hopper and his ancestry.

The old man almost grinned. "Must of been one of them who escaped from the First World."

"Who?"

"One of the Grasshopper People."

I looked around and moved closer. "The Grasshopper People? Who were the Grasshopper People?"

Minutes passed. "What you call insects? Bugs."

I would later learn that he was sort of testing me because I'd taken a book on the Zuni from the car and was thumbing through it. He recognized the subject of the book.

"Where did they come from?" I asked, finally.

He looked at me for a long time without exactly looking at me. It's a gift obviously given only to the Navajo because I still know no other people who can come close to doing it so well.

"That car come from overseas?" he asked.

"Yes, Germany."

More time passed. Billie Begay cursed some more. "My

brother was overseas. Fighting Jappie." He almost smiled.

"A codetalker?" I asked. At least I knew that much.

He nodded.

"You want one of these drinks?" I asked.

He smiled.

"Now about these Grasshopper People? You say the grasshoppers came from the First World?

"Some say that. I don't."

Well, I finally got him to say more about the Grasshopper People. In the days that followed he told me a great deal about the Grasshopper People. He was a kind, sharing man. Perhaps it started because I kept his nephew, Billie Begay, from killing himself that night.

That was in Gallup. Billie Begay found the foreign car man for me and the second worst motel in Gallup which was just up the street from an Indian bar. The Esquire Lounge. Skip a few hours and I wander in to see what the party is all about. And there sits Billie Begay, as drunk as any man I'd ever seen. And I've, suddenly, become his best friend in the world. Billie Begay couldn't drive. Billie Begay couldn't walk. I didn't want to see a fine swearing man like Billie Begay kill himself and my motel room was so miserable that it made no difference where I slept anyway, so about two o'clock in the morning I drove Billie Begay back across the state line and spent my first night ever in a hogan. Old Man Manuelito Begay did not seem the least bit surprised when he found me sleeping in one of his hogans the next morning. He just started talking right about where he'd left off the afternoon before. It was the beginning of a wonderful journey for me; a learning experience that continues to this day.

"So you want talk of Grasshopper People?"

"Especially Grasshopper People."

He glanced at me, looked away, then nodded. "You

have a long time? Some people don't like for a story to take a long time."

I certainly had a lot of time, as it turned out.

He nodded. "The First World was a hot place, much like this, where summer winds stirred up the dust circles. There was little grass, so there were no cattle, deer, not even birds, not even the little ga (the cottontail rabbit) or the ga'tso (jackrabbit), not the ma'i (coyote), were in that First World."

I started to interrupt, to get ahead of him by asking what was in that first world. He held up his hand to quiet me. "You have turquoise?" he asked.

I didn't have turquoise.

He removed a small bracelet from his arm and handed it to me. "You listen with that," he instructed. Somehow I knew what he meant.

We became good friends. And I became good friends with Billie Begay who now lives in Los Angeles but is constantly returning for Ways. He should have become a Singer. A swearing Singer.

I'm not sure that Singer Begay wasn't pulling my leg when he told me the story of the Man Who Killed Santa Claus. However it is really a very "Navajo" story, although it really isn't considered a "polite" story by Navajos; not one many people would repeat to non-Navajos, as it could be interpreted as poking fun at Bilagaana customs and religions as it revolves around a Christian missioniary. I've only known a few Navajos who've heard the story and others I've asked about it recently—Elizabeth Sells, Vern and Shirley Teller—have never heard it. It could be entirely hypothetical but I prefer not to think so; Christian missionaries have been making fools of themselves since they were first sent to Dinetah shortly after the 1868 peace treaty. They're still there and will continue to arrive yearly, no doubt. Too, the attitude toward the "event" and death of Santa Claus is just too in character for a people who have long since gotten over being surprised at the seemingly endless lengths to which white people will go to convince others that they own the "right way" and the only way in religious matters.

There was a Christian Missionary sent from one of the more fundamental sects back east. He and his family had been on the reservation for some years, working the area between Gallup and Window Rock. His people back east kept sending him money, old clothing and gifts of food to hand out to the "poor" Navajos but the only time he could get anyone to show up at his tiny little church on Sunday was when he had goods to pass out. The local Navajos just were not too pleasantly moved by his "fire and brimstone" sermons and tales of a dead Christ coming back to life.

Since the Missionary was getting nowhere with his job of converting the Navajo to "Christ and the American Way of Life," he decided drastic and dramatic deeds were called for. He gave the matter a lot of thought and since it was nearing Christmas, came up with the idea of bringing Santa Claus to the Navajos. He called his people back east and told them what he was about to do and asked them to donate a lot of gift-wrapped toys for the event, which they did.

Then he posted signs all over that portion of the reservation telling the Navajos that on Christmas Eve Santa Claus would come down out of the sky to a certain pasture between Window Rock and Gallup and distribute gifts to all the children.

He'd arranged to hire a small plane from Gallup and a former paratrooper who would play Santa Claus, parachute out of the plane with a bag of toys and hand out all the gifts he'd gotten from back east.

When Christmas Eve rolled around the former paratrooper showed up too drunk to walk, much less jump out of an airplane. And several hundred Navajos had gathered to see Santa Claus come down out of the sky. The Missionary was beside himself, until the pilot got the idea of stuffing the Santa Claus suit with straw and dropping it out of the plane himself, having faith the chute would open.

Well, of course, the chute did not open; Santa Claus came out the sky like a bowling ball, hit the ground with a splat, and that was that. The gathering of Navajos gave a collective shrug, having not expected much more in the first place, and went home. But forever after the Missionary was known to the Navajos as "The Man Who Killed Santa Claus."

Recently, I told this tale to Vern and Shirley Teller and Vern told me another tale that has been around Navajoland for a few decades. It took place somewhere up around Navajo Mountain in the days when thirty dollars would buy a good horse.

This old Navajo man owned a beautiful horse, and one day he was visited by a local trader who saw the horse for the first time and decided he had to own the animal and was sure, considering the time and place, he would get it cheap.

"That is a beautiful horse you got there," the trader said.

The old Navajo stared at the horse. "Naw, he don't look so good."

"I don't know about that," the trader disagreed, "he's a beautiful animal but considering he looks wild and dangerous, I'm only willing to give you ten dollars for him."

"I don't want to sell that horse. Anyway, he don't look

so good."

"Okay, okay," said the trader. "I'll give you twenty five dollars for that horse. Not that I think he's worth it but I have to admit he is a beautiful horse."

The old Navajo thought about this a while, walked over and looked the horse over. "Twenty five dollars is a lot of money but I don't think I can sell him to you. Anyway, he don't look so good."

"That's it, you old rascal. I've heard that you're one hellva horse trader. Now this is my last offer. I'll give you fifty dollars for that horse and that is that. It is my last offer and that's only because that's the best looking horse I've seen in years."

The old Navajo looked from the horse to the trader to the horse. "For a horse that don't look so good that's a lot of money," the old Navajo said. "I guess you want him so much I'll take your fifty dollars."

The trader took the horse and led him away, trailing after the one he'd ridden there. But in about three days he was back. And very upset.

"You owe me fifty dollars!" he said to the old Navajo.

The old Navajo stared past the trader. "How come you say I owe you fifty dollars?"

"That horse you sold me is blind!"

The old Navajo looked off into the distance for a long time. "I thought maybe a smart white trader must know how to fix that horse because I told you four times he don't look so good."

Raymond Friday Locke is the author of the highly acclaimed **The Book of the Navajo** which, in December of 1989, was published in a fourth edition. It is considered the definitive work on the Navajo and is used in the tribal run college system to teach Navajo students Navajo social, cultural and military history, as well as in many other colleges and universities. Mr. Locke has published extensively in the field of Native American studies. His first book for Roundtable was the novel, **Seldom Sung Songs,** which was critically praised.

The Critics Say:

The Book of the Navajo

"Locke writes splendidly; this is history laced with data, you-are-there commentary and poetic symbolism. He rarely minces words."
The Boston Globe

"The Book of the Navajo is beautifully written and gives a much needed view unfettered by anthropological conjecture."
Dr. Ray Brandes,
Chairman, Department of History
University of San Diego

Joaquin Murietta

"A splendid piece of work. Locke backs his tale of the folk hero Joaquin Murietta with solid historical research. I loved every page of it.
William Lewis
Professor, Spanish Studies
UC Santa Barbara
Mankind Magazine

Seldom Sung Songs

"Ray Locke writes with a poignant pen of his native Mississippi."
New York Tribune

"Mr. Locke's terse, narrative voice is one that merits listening to."
The New York Times Book Review

"No matter your geographical or sociological background, the sorrow, envy, mistaken loyalty, corrosive ambition, failure and despair here are universal experiences touching innermost recesses of mind and heart . . . Superior reading.
Pittsburg Press